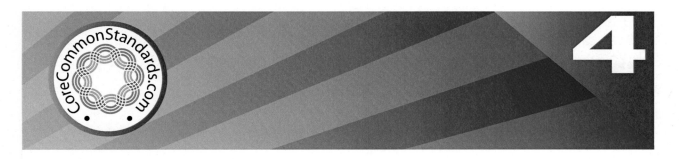

Common Core State Standards

4

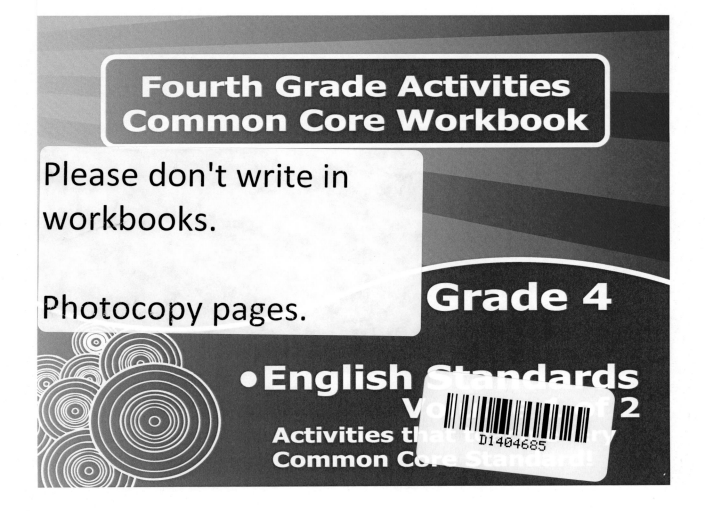

Fourth Grade Activities
Common Core Workbook

Please don't write in workbooks.

Photocopy pages.

Grade 4

English Standards
Volume 1 of 2
Activities that teach every
Common Core Standard!

Table of Contents

English Language Arts

Answer Key

4

Common Core State Standards

Fourth Grade Activities
Common Core Workbook

Grade 4

• English Standards

Activities that teach every Common Core Standard!

Use the text to make inferences

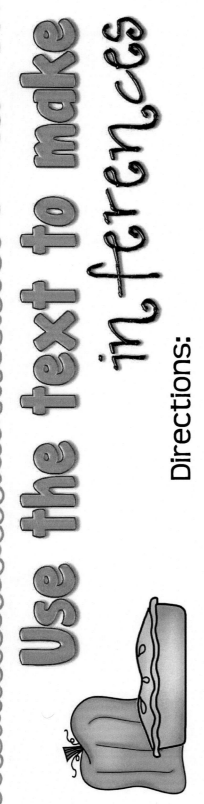

Directions:

Refer to details and examples in a text when explaining what the text says explicitly and when drawing inferences from the text.

Read "Pumpkin Pies" and graphic organizer to make inferences and to show what the text says explicitly.

Students can use the same graphic organizer as they read any text to practice finding the answer in the text.

Standard: English Language Arts| Reading: Literature| RL.4.1
Graphics by Scrappin Doodles www.CoreCommonStandards.com

This is a Blank Page

You May Cut Out Resources On Back

This is a Blank Page

We use ....

What the character says

What the character does

What the author writes

to make inferences

Standard: English Language Arts| Reading:- Literature| RL.4.1 ww.CoreCommonStandards.com

This is a Blank Page

You May Cut Out Resources On Back

This is a Blank Page

Pumpkin Pies
Story By: Judie Eberhardt

Halloween was over, and Jessie was wondering what to do with all the pumpkins she had left over from the holiday. It was a shame to throw them away. They were still in good shape. I know she thought to herself, I will make some pumpkin pies.

That night Jessie gathered all the ingredients she needed to make her pie. She rolled out the dough, mashed up the pumpkin, and made sure all the pumpkin seeds were taken out. She added some cinnamon and nutmeg as her spices. When she was ready, she put the pie in the oven. "Wow!" said mom when she came into the kitchen. "That sure smells yummy!" "I can't wait for the pies to finish," said Jessie. "I want to take some pie to Mrs. Johnson." Mrs. Johnson was Jessie's next door neighbor who lived alone and didn't get much company.

The pies were finally finished baking, and Jessie took two slices of pie to Mrs. Johnson. "Oh Jessie, this pie is so delicious!" "Thank you for bringing me some." "My church would enjoy these pies for their carnival coming up next Saturday," said Mrs. Johnson. "I have two more pumpkins," said Jessie. "Would you like me to make two pies?" she asked. "That would be wonderful," said Mrs. Johnson.

Jessie made her pumpkin pies, and they sold at the church carnival within the first hour the carnival was open. Many people that bought the pies wanted to know where they could buy more of the pies that were sold at the carnival. Mrs. Johnson told them her young neighbor had made them, but she didn't know if she was interested in baking anymore, now that the "pumpkin season" was coming to an end.

Jessie took orders for more pies after church the next weekend, and she began making pies for special events. She made pies for a baby shower, a birthday party, and even a pie for a child that made all A's on his report card. Jessie was so proud of her pies, and her parents were even more proud. Jessie continued to make pies for people that had a different event or party. Jessie became known as the "Pumpkin Princess" among her friends.

Standard: English Language Arts| Reading: Literature| RL.4.1 ww.CoreCommonStandards.com

This is a Blank Page

You May Cut Out Resources On Back

This is a Blank Page

Name: _____

Inferences
What do we learn about Jessie?

From the text	
It's a shame to throw them away. They were still in good shape.	
Mrs. Johnson was Jessie's next door neighborhood who lived alone and didn't get much company.	
"Oh Jessie, this pie is so delicious!"	
She made pies for a baby shower, a birthday party, and even a pie for a child that made all A's on his report card.	
Jessie became known as the "Pumpkin Princess" among her friends.	

Standard: English Language Arts| Reading: Literature| RL.4.1   www.CoreCommonStandards.com

This is a Blank Page

You May Cut Out Resources On Back

This is a Blank Page

Name: _____

From the text

Inferences
What do we learn about _____?

Standard: English Language Arts | Reading: Literature | RL.4.1

This is a Blank Page

You May Cut Out Resources On Back

This is a Blank Page

INFERENCE CHAINS

DIRECTIONS:
  Choose a story. Using the evidence chains, make an inference about an event in the story, a character, or even what might happen next. Then fill in the next two links with an exact quote from the story that supports your thinking and another supporting detail.
  You can always compare your thinking with a neighbor.

Refer to details and examples in a text when explaining what the text says explicitly and when drawing inferences from the text.

Standard: English Language Arts | Reading: Literature | RL.4.1

www.CoreCommonStandards.com

This is a Blank Page

You May Cut Out Resources On Back

This is a Blank Page

BUILD YOUR EVIDENCE CHAINS

INFERENCE LINK

INFERENCE LINK

QUOTE LINK

QUOTE LINK

SUPPORTING DETAIL LINK

SUPPORTING DETAIL LINK

This is a Blank Page

You May Cut Out Resources On Back

This is a Blank Page

BUILD YOUR EVIDENCE CHAINS

INFERENCE LINK

QUOTE LINK

SUPPORTING DETAIL LINK

INFERENCE LINK

QUOTE LINK

SUPPORTING DETAIL LINK

This is a Blank Page

You May Cut Out Resources On Back

This is a Blank Page

Determining Theme

Graphics: Scrappin Doodles

Directions:
Determine a theme of a story, drama, or poem from details in the text; summarize the text.

Standard: English Language Arts l Reading Literature l RL.4.2

www.CoreCommonStandards.com

This is a Blank Page

You May Cut Out Resources On Back

This is a Blank Page

Pick Me!
Story By: Andrew Frinkle

Eddie really liked to play dodgeball. He was not the tallest kid, and he was not the biggest kid. He was not the fastest kid, and he was not the slowest kid. He was the kid with the best hands.

When his classmates chose teammates for dodgeball, they liked to pick the fast kids first, because they were good at dodging. Then they would pick the kids with the strong arms, because they were good at getting people out when they threw a ball. Everyone else came after that.

Eddie usually got picked last, and it made him sad. Maybe if he was taller or faster, it would have helped. He couldn't help that, but he could do his best. He would have to show them that his talents made for a good team.

When the game started, the fast kids ran forward and grabbed the balls first. They threw them, and several people on each team were eliminated. Then, the strong arms came in handy. The boys with the best arms could whiz the dodgeballs across the court. It stung if one of them hit you.

Some of the big kids went down first. They made easy targets. The fast kids fell eventually, too. That left Eddie standing alone on the court for his team, holding a red rubber ball.

www.CoreCommonStandards.com   Standard: English Language Arts | Reading Literature | RL.4.2

This is a Blank Page

You May Cut Out Resources On Back

This is a Blank Page

He smiled, even though his teammates groaned to see him facing four enemies on his own. "Not Eddie." They whined, thinking he was useless, but he would show them.

When one of the strong arms on the other team threw a ball, he deflected it with his own and tagged him out with his ball. Now there were only three left on the other team. The odds were more even now.

He got another ball and approached the center line. A fast kid charged at him, throwing the ball low.

Eddie dropped his own ball and caught the other kid's ball. The fast kid was out, and he got one of his teammates back. "John, you're in!" Eddie shouted over his shoulder.

Everyone watched in surprise. Now it was two-on-two. Eddie and John each got a ball, sighted in the slow kid on the other team and fired. Eddie missed, but his shot led the other player right into John's shot. Now it was two-to-one.

It didn't take long to finish off the last kid. Eddie was a hero. His team rushed in to cheer for him. They wouldn't be picking him last anymore.

This is a Blank Page

You May Cut Out Resources On Back

This is a Blank Page

Determining Theme

Theme:

Evidence from the Text:

Summary:

_____

_____

_____

_____

_____

www.CoreCommonStandards.com   Standard: English Language Arts | Reading Literature | RL.4.2

This is a Blank Page

You May Cut Out Resources On Back

This is a Blank Page

IDENTIFYING THEMES

DIRECTIONS:

Choose a poem, a play, or a story. Fill in at least two of the cloud cards. Choose the ones that seem most fitting for the piece you read. They will help you determine the themes. Blank cards have been provided for you to make your own questions, too.

Share your findings with someone else who has read the same piece. Did you agree?

Determine a theme of a story, drama, or poem from details in the text; summarize the text.

Standard: English Language Arts | Reading: Literature | RL.4.2

This is a Blank Page

You May Cut Out Resources On Back

This is a Blank Page

CLOUD CARDS

What did you learn about the characters?

What did you notice that was special about the words used?

How did the piece make you feel?

What lessons did you learn?

This is a Blank Page

You May Cut Out Resources On Back

This is a Blank Page

CLOUD CARDS

How did things change between the beginning and the end?

Were there any surprises during the piece?

What character or part of the piece did the writer seem to focus on most?

Was the writer trying to persuade you, to make you feel something, or to inform you of something? Explain.

This is a Blank Page

You May Cut Out Resources On Back

This is a Blank Page

BLANK CLOUD CARDS

23

This is a Blank Page

You May Cut Out Resources On Back

This is a Blank Page

Welcome to the Neighborhood

Directions:
Describe in depth a character, setting, or event in a story or drama, drawing on specific details in the text (e.g., a character's thoughts, words, or actions).

Standard: English Language Arts | Literature | 4.RL.3

www.CoreCommonStandards.com

Graphics: Scrappin Doodles

This is a Blank Page

You May Cut Out Resources On Back

This is a Blank Page

Welcome to the Neighborhood
Story By: Judie Eberhardt

The old Roger house had been empty for six months, and finally someone was moving in. Betsy didn't see any children getting out of the car, just an older woman in a wheelchair. Betsy thought, she is going to be lonely by herself. The moving men brought all the furniture into the house. The lady didn't have too many things. Betsy started feeling sorry for her. "Mom, is it alright if I go over to say hello to our new neighbor?" "Why don't you wait until tomorrow?" "Give her a chance to get settled."

The next morning they decided to bring some cookies to their new neighbor and introduce themselves. The lady came to the door and said her name was Emily Harris. She invited them into the house. "Please forgive the way the house looks," said Miss Harris. "I haven't had much time to put things away and being in a wheelchair makes it twice as hard." Betsy and her mom introduced themselves and stayed only for a short time. "We don't want to hold you up," said Betsy's mom. "If you ever need anything, let us know." "Thanks so much," said Miss Harris.

After breakfast the next day, Betsy decided she wanted to help Miss Harris get settled in. It was Saturday, so she had all day. Betsy really liked Miss Harris. Betsy rang the doorbell but didn't get an answer. The door was unlocked, so Betsy peeked in only to see Miss Harris had tried to reach a shelf and had taken a fall next to her wheelchair. Betsy ran to Miss Harris and asked her if she was alright. "I think I broke my arm," said Miss Harris. "I'll be right back," said Betsy.

She ran home and told her mom. They called for an ambulance. They arrived shortly and took Miss Harris to the hospital. While Miss Harris was gone, Betsy decided to unpack the boxes that were on the floor and put things away to surprise and help Miss Harris once she returned home. She was going to need a lot of help now that she broke her arm. When Miss Harris returned home on Sunday, she was surprised by Betsy's hard work. "You are a very kind girl," said Miss Harris. "I'm so lucky to have bought this house next to you!" Betsy smiled the biggest smile and said, "Welcome to the neighborhood."

www.CoreCommonStandards.com   Standard: English Language Arts | Literature | RL.4.3

This is a Blank Page

You May Cut Out Resources On Back

This is a Blank Page

Character Sketch

Using evidence from the text, describe the character. Use the character's actions, thoughts, and words to help you.

Character:
_____

Picture of the character:

This is a Blank Page

You May Cut Out Resources On Back

This is a Blank Page

Greek Mythology

Characters, Words, and Phrases

Directions

Match the Character Cards with the Words and Phrases Cards. Use the blank Character Cards to create your own. Then, complete the practice worksheet. You can also use the Character Maps to write words and phrases that allude to the characters.

Standard

Determine the meaning of words and phrases as they are used in a text, including those that allude to significant characters found in mythology (e.g., Herculean).

Standard: English Language Arts | Reading: Literature | RL.4.4

This is a Blank Page

You May Cut Out Resources On Back

This is a Blank Page

Hercules

Herculean

mighty

Achilles

Achilles' Heel

a person's weak spot

This is a Blank Page

You May Cut Out Resources On Back

This is a Blank Page

Athena

Atheneum

wisdom

King Midas

Midas touch

a person who is always lucky

This is a Blank Page

You May Cut Out Resources On Back

This is a Blank Page

Icarus

wings of wax

don't fly too close to the sun

Medusa

with one look, you turn to stone

a severely ugly woman

This is a Blank Page

You May Cut Out Resources On Back

This is a Blank Page

Orpheus

Orphic poems

poet and musician

Odysseus

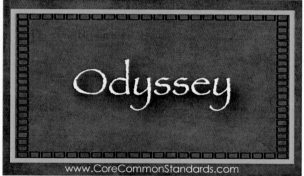

Odyssey

adventure or journey

This is a Blank Page

You May Cut Out Resources On Back

This is a Blank Page

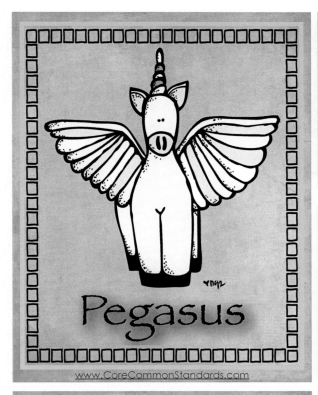

Pegasus

winged horse

my Pegasus will not go this morning

Zeus

father and ruler of the Olympians

Mount Olympus

This is a Blank Page

You May Cut Out Resources On Back

This is a Blank Page

www.CoreCommonStandards.com

www.CoreCommonStandards.com

www.CoreCommonStandards.com

www.CoreCommonStandards.com

www.CoreCommonStandards.com

www.CoreCommonStandards.com

This is a Blank Page

You May Cut Out Resources On Back

This is a Blank Page

Name: _____

Greek Mythology

Character	Words and Phrases

Hercules	→ _____ _____
Achilles	→ _____ _____
Athena	→ _____ _____
King Midas	→ _____ _____
Icarus	→ _____ _____
Medusa	→ _____ _____
Orpheus	→ _____ _____
Odysseus	→ _____ _____
Pegasus	→ _____ _____
Zeus	→ _____ _____

This is a Blank Page

You May Cut Out Resources On Back

This is a Blank Page

Hercules

www.CoreCommonStandards.com

This is a Blank Page

You May Cut Out Resources On Back

This is a Blank Page

Achilles

www.CoreCommonStandards.com

This is a Blank Page

You May Cut Out Resources On Back

This is a Blank Page

Athena

www.CoreCommonStandards.com

This is a Blank Page

You May Cut Out Resources On Back

This is a Blank Page

King Midas

www.CoreCommonStandards.com

This is a Blank Page

You May Cut Out Resources On Back

This is a Blank Page

Icarus

www.CoreCommonStandards.com

This is a Blank Page

You May Cut Out Resources On Back

This is a Blank Page

Medusa

www.CoreCommonStandards.com

This is a Blank Page

You May Cut Out Resources On Back

This is a Blank Page

Orpheus

www.CoreCommonStandards.com

This is a Blank Page

You May Cut Out Resources On Back

This is a Blank Page

Odysseus

www.CoreCommonStandards.com

This is a Blank Page

You May Cut Out Resources On Back

This is a Blank Page

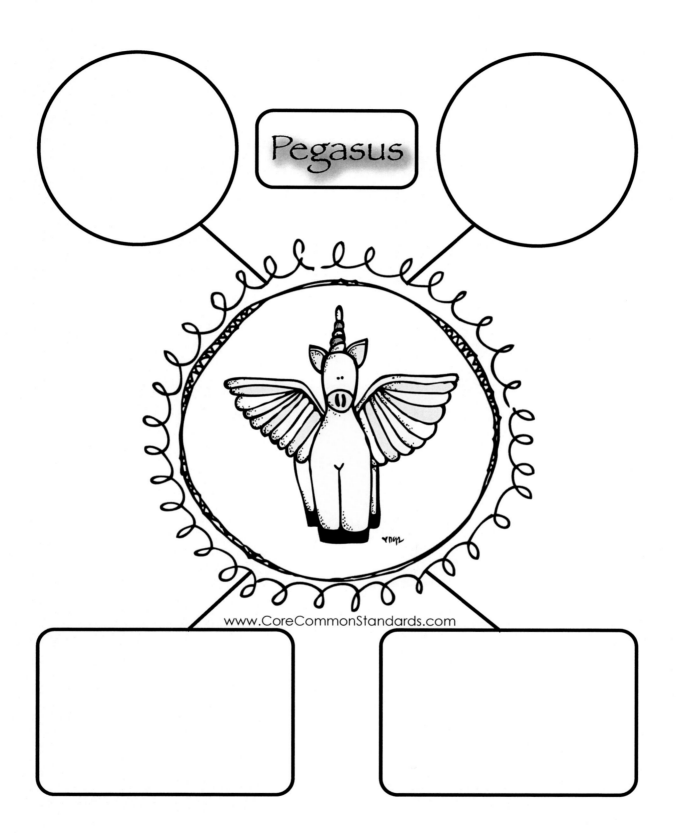

Pegasus

www.CoreCommonStandards.com

This is a Blank Page

You May Cut Out Resources On Back

This is a Blank Page

Zeus

www.CoreCommonStandards.com

This is a Blank Page

You May Cut Out Resources On Back

This is a Blank Page

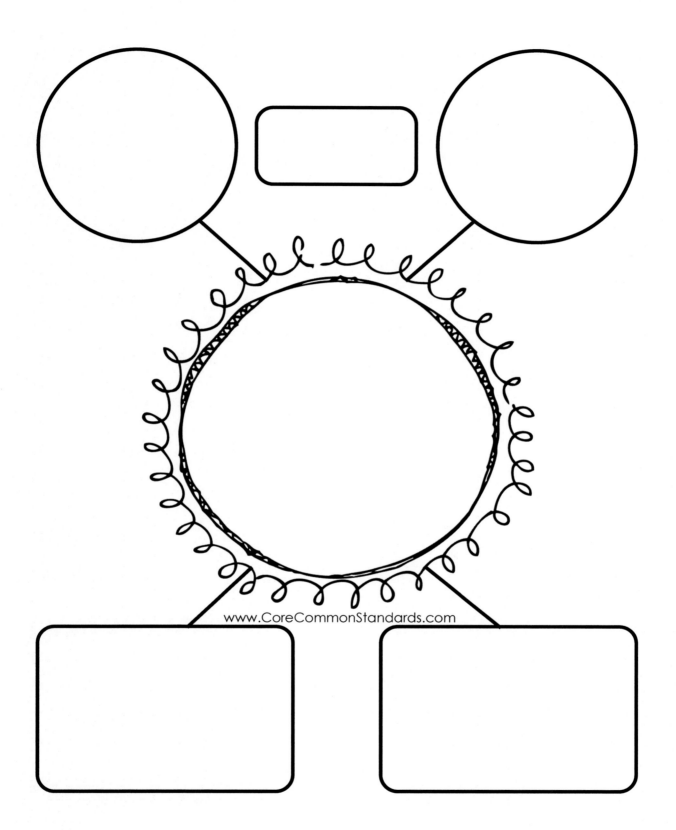

www.CoreCommonStandards.com

This is a Blank Page

You May Cut Out Resources On Back

This is a Blank Page

Three Amigos
Poetry, Prose, and Drama

Directions: Sort the word cards by genre (prose, poetry, and drama). Use the sorted cards to label and fill out a Venn diagram.
Use the color-coded activity cards and organizers for beginners, and use the blue activity cards and black organizers for advanced.

Standard: Explain major differences between poems, drama, and prose, and refer to the structural elements of poems (e.g., verse, rhythm, meter) and drama (e.g., casts of characters, settings, descriptions, dialogue, stage directions) when writing or speaking about a text.

Standard: English Language Arts | Reading: Literature | RL.4.5
Graphics by ScrappinDoodles   www.CoreCommonStandards.com

This is a Blank Page

You May Cut Out Resources On Back

This is a Blank Page

Standard: English Language Arts | Reading: Literature | RL.4.5

www.CoreCommonStandards.com

This is a Blank Page

You May Cut Out Resources On Back

This is a Blank Page

Drama

	scene
cast of characters	act
setting	monologue
stage directions	mood
dialogue	description

This is a Blank Page

You May Cut Out Resources On Back

This is a Blank Page

Poetry

	couplet
meter	mood
rhythm	rhyme
verse	stanza
rhyme scheme	voice

This is a Blank Page

You May Cut Out Resources On Back

This is a Blank Page

Prose	**dialogue**
character	**chapter**
narration	**voice**
paragraph	**setting**
point of view	**plot**

This is a Blank Page

You May Cut Out Resources On Back

This is a Blank Page

Drama

	scene
cast of characters	act
setting	monologue
stage directions	mood
dialogue	description

This is a Blank Page

You May Cut Out Resources On Back

This is a Blank Page

Poetry

	couplet
meter	**mood**
rhythm	**rhyme**
	www.CoreCommonStandards.com
verse	**stanza**
rhyme scheme	**voice**

This is a Blank Page

You May Cut Out Resources On Back

This is a Blank Page

Prose	**dialogue**
character	**chapter**
narration	**voice**
paragraph	**setting**
point of view	**plot**

This is a Blank Page

You May Cut Out Resources On Back

This is a Blank Page

Name_____

Directions: After sorting the cards on the activity mat, use the words to label and fill in the Venn diagram.

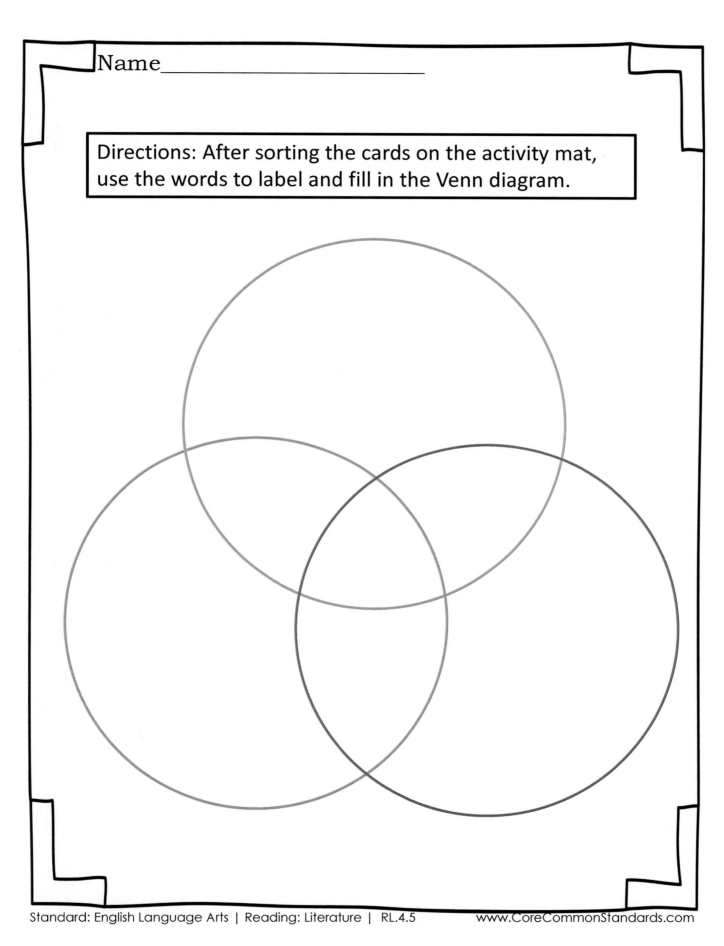

This is a Blank Page

You May Cut Out Resources On Back

This is a Blank Page

Name_____

Directions: After sorting the cards on the activity mat, use the words to label and fill in the Venn diagram.

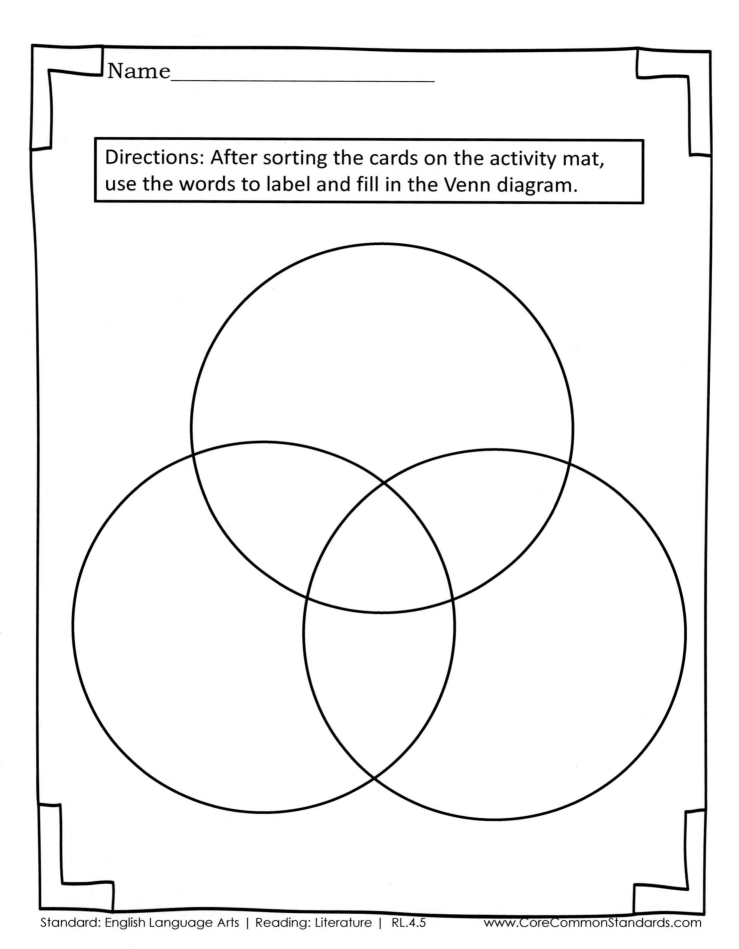

This is a Blank Page

You May Cut Out Resources On Back

This is a Blank Page

Name_____

Directions: After sorting the cards on the activity mat, use the words to label and fill in the Venn diagram.

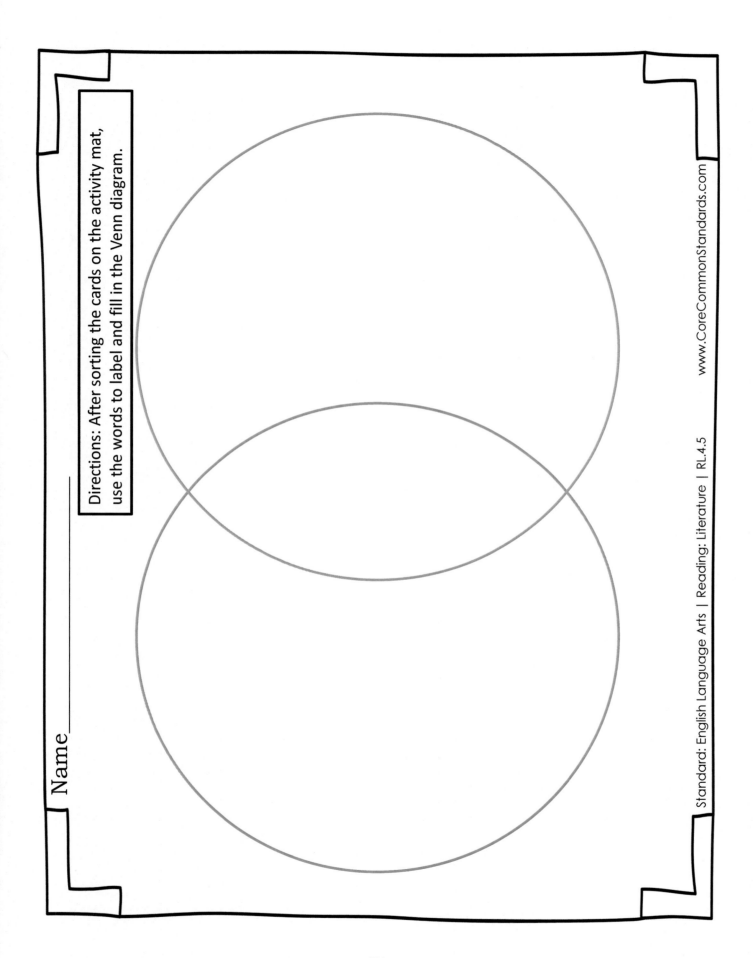

Standard: English Language Arts | Reading: Literature | RL.4.5   www.CoreCommonStandards.com

This is a Blank Page

You May Cut Out Resources On Back

This is a Blank Page

Name

Directions: After sorting the cards on the activity mat, use the words to label and fill in the Venn diagram.

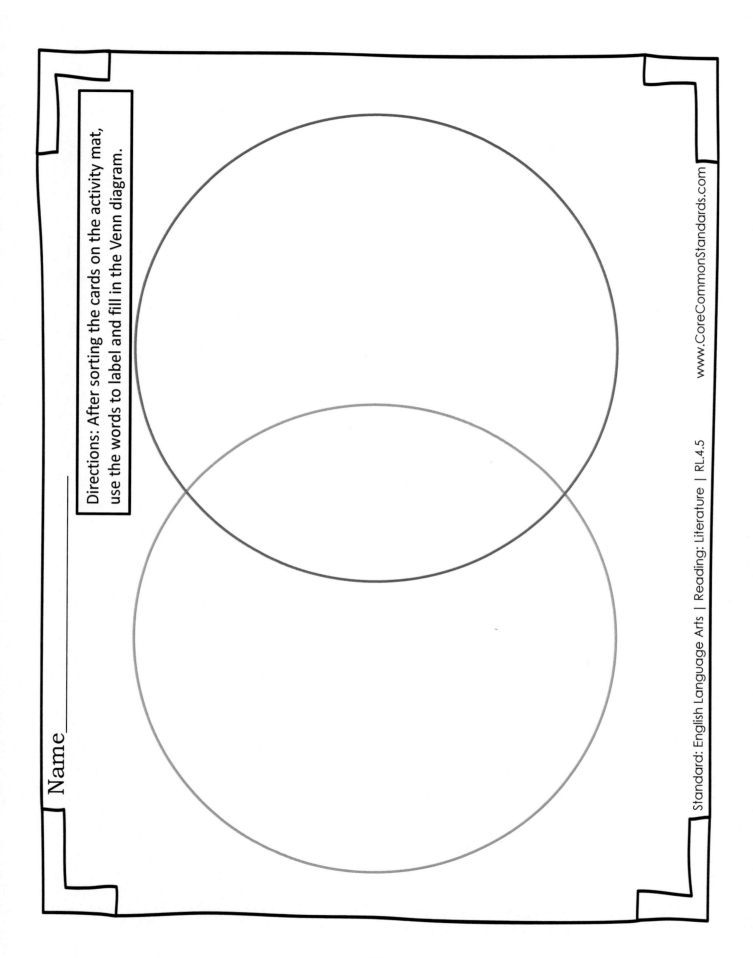

Standard: English Language Arts | Reading: Literature | RL.4.5   www.CoreCommonStandards.com

This is a Blank Page

You May Cut Out Resources On Back

This is a Blank Page

Name _____

Directions: After sorting the cards on the activity mat, use the words to label and fill in the Venn diagram.

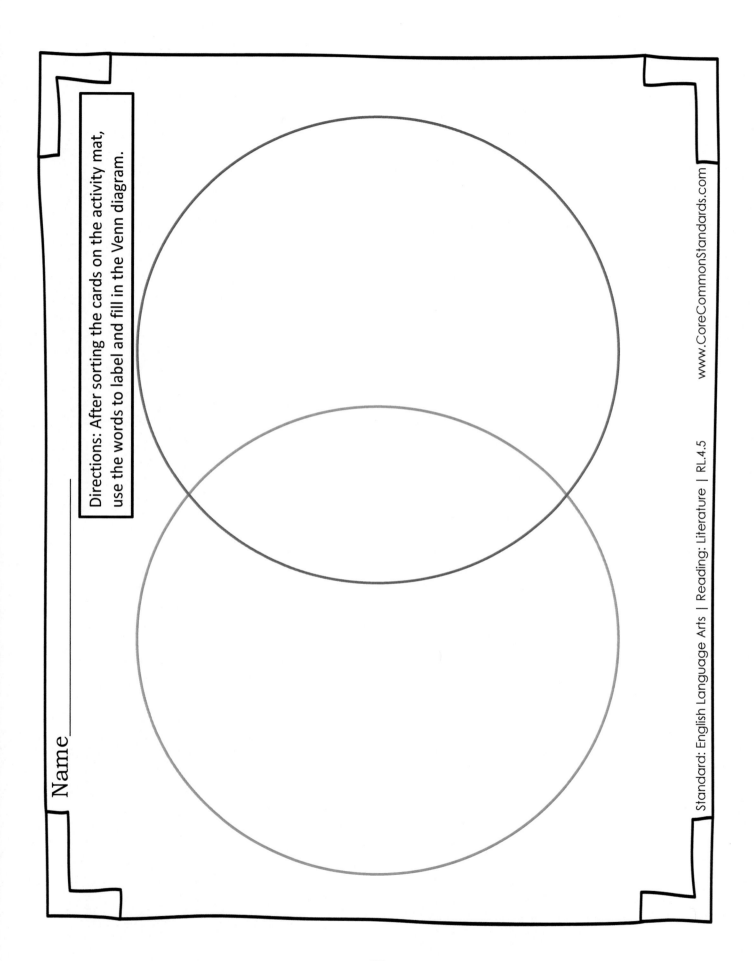

Standard: English Language Arts | Reading: Literature | RL.4.5

www.CoreCommonStandards.com

This is a Blank Page

You May Cut Out Resources On Back

This is a Blank Page

Name _____

Directions: After sorting the cards on the activity mat, use the words to label and fill in the Venn diagram.

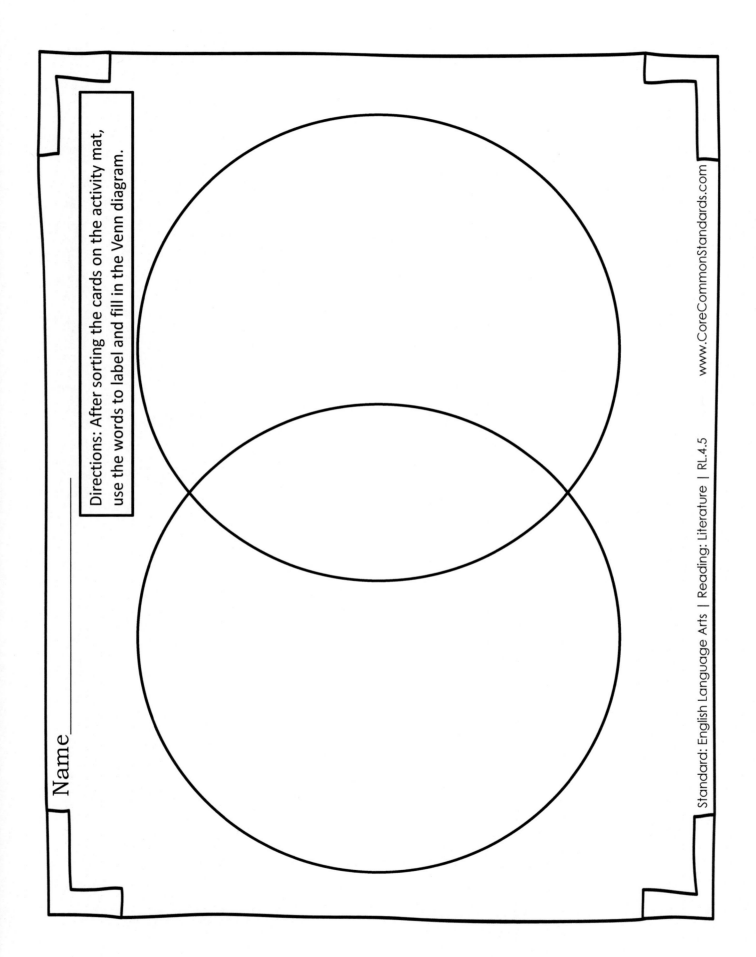

Standard: English Language Arts | Reading: Literature | RL.4.5   www.CoreCommonStandards.com

This is a Blank Page

You May Cut Out Resources On Back

This is a Blank Page

IDENTIFYING LITERARY ELEMENTS

DIRECTIONS:
Choose a poem, a play, and a story. Fill in the provided literary elements cards with details from the literary pieces that seem the most fitting. Then cut them out and sort them into piles, depending on what kind of writing they describe best. Make sure to use quotes and details from the writing as you fill in the cards.

Explain major differences between poems, drama, and prose, and refer to the structural elements of poems (e.g., verse, rhythm, meter) and drama (e.g., casts of characters, settings, descriptions, dialogue, stage directions) when writing or speaking about a text.

Standard: English Language Arts | Reading: Literature | RL.4.5

www.CoreCommonStandards.com

This is a Blank Page

You May Cut Out Resources On Back

This is a Blank Page

LITERARY ELEMENTS CARDS

SETTING:

SETTING:

VERSE:

RHYTHM:

CHARACTERS:

CHARACTERS:

This is a Blank Page

You May Cut Out Resources On Back

This is a Blank Page

LITERARY ELEMENTS CARDS

RHYMING:

STAGE DIRECTIONS:

METER:

THEME:

DIALOGUE:

DIALOGUE:

This is a Blank Page

You May Cut Out Resources On Back

This is a Blank Page

PLAY ELEMENTS CARDS

STORY ELEMENTS CARDS

POETRY ELEMENTS CARDS

This is a Blank Page

You May Cut Out Resources On Back

This is a Blank Page

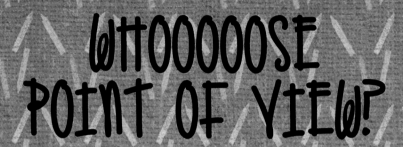

WHOOOOOSE POINT OF VIEW?

Directions:
Compare and contrast the point of view from which different stories are narrated, including the difference between first- and third-person narration. Sort the story cards under the correct point of view tree.

Standard: English | Reading Literature | RL.4.6

www.CoreCommonStandards.com

Graphics: Scrappin Doodles

This is a Blank Page

You May Cut Out Resources On Back

This is a Blank Page

FIRST PERSON POINT OF VIEW

THIRD PERSON POINT OF VIEW

www.CoreCommonStandards.com   Standard: English I Reading Literature I RL.4.6

This is a Blank Page

You May Cut Out Resources On Back

This is a Blank Page

E. As he walked down the hall, he wondered about his classmates. How awful would they be? They would probably be wild, like gorillas battling for control of the jungle.

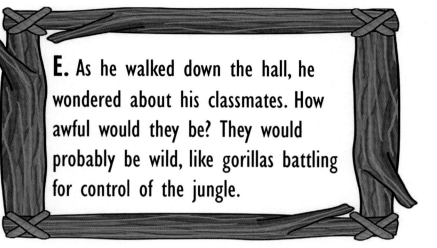

F. That night Jessie gathered all the ingredients she needed to make her pie. She rolled out the dough, mashed up the pumpkin, and made sure all the pumpkin seeds were taken out.

H. As the classes neared their end, some twenty lessons later, Tara was delighted to hear she'd been selected as a finalist.

This is a Blank Page

You May Cut Out Resources On Back

This is a Blank Page

L. Casey sighed. It was hard to remember it all. "It's a little confusing, but I think I get it

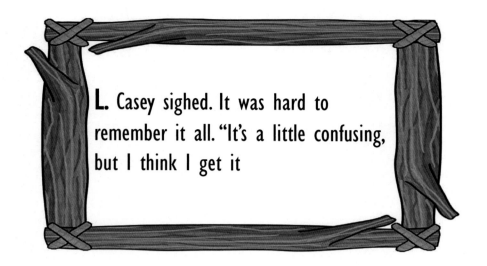

A. He liked to train them, so he'd adopted Herschel. If it was going to work out, it would take lots of patience, love, and training.

G. Many people think that we are the only creatures that look to the stars and see pictures, but there are others that look up and see things.

www.CoreCommonStandards.com

This is a Blank Page

You May Cut Out Resources On Back

This is a Blank Page

D. I usually got picked last, and it made me sad. Maybe if I was taller or faster, it would have helped. I can't help that, but I could do his best.

I. She wanted to play, but I didn't want to. In my defense, I *did look very tired.* "Why won't you play with me?"

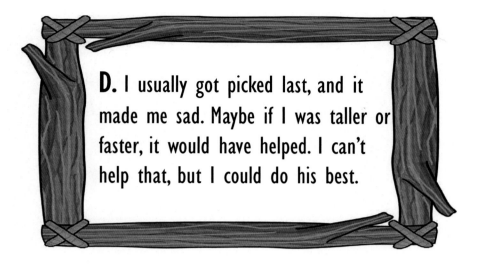

C. I sighed as my mother pulled up in the car loop to get me after school. My mother's grey minivan stood out in a crowd of shiny SUV's and sharp- looking new sedans.

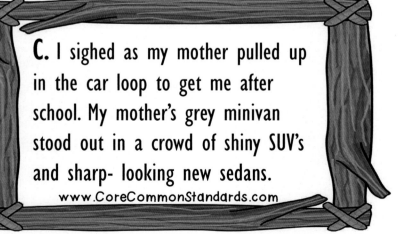

www.CoreCommonStandards.com

This is a Blank Page

You May Cut Out Resources On Back

This is a Blank Page

B. There it was. My sister's favorite character was a pink lizard with goofy eyes. It was from '*A Lizard's Tail.*' I looked at the price of Pokey the Pink Lizard.

J. Joe laughed at the back of the classroom. What he was doing wasn't really that funny, but it was fun to laugh really loud.

K. I am terrified of the dark. In fact, I can't sleep without leaving the lights on.

This is a Blank Page

You May Cut Out Resources On Back

This is a Blank Page

WHOOOOOSE POINT OF VIEW?

Write the letter on the story card
under the correct tree.

FIRST PERSON POINT OF VIEW

THIRD PERSON POINT OF VIEW

This is a Blank Page

You May Cut Out Resources On Back

This is a Blank Page

WHOOOOOSE POINT OF VIEW?
Write the letter on the story card
under the correct tree.

FIRST PERSON POINT OF VIEW

B, C, D, G, I, K

THIRD PERSON POINT OF VIEW

A, E, F, H, J, L

This is a Blank Page

You May Cut Out Resources On Back

This is a Blank Page

book vs. movie

directions:
make connections between the text of a story or drama and a visual or oral presentation of the text. fill in the graphic organizer with similarities and differences.

Standard: English Language Arts | Literature | 4.RL.7

www.CoreCommonStandards.com

Graphics: Scrappin Doodles

This is a Blank Page

You May Cut Out Resources On Back

This is a Blank Page

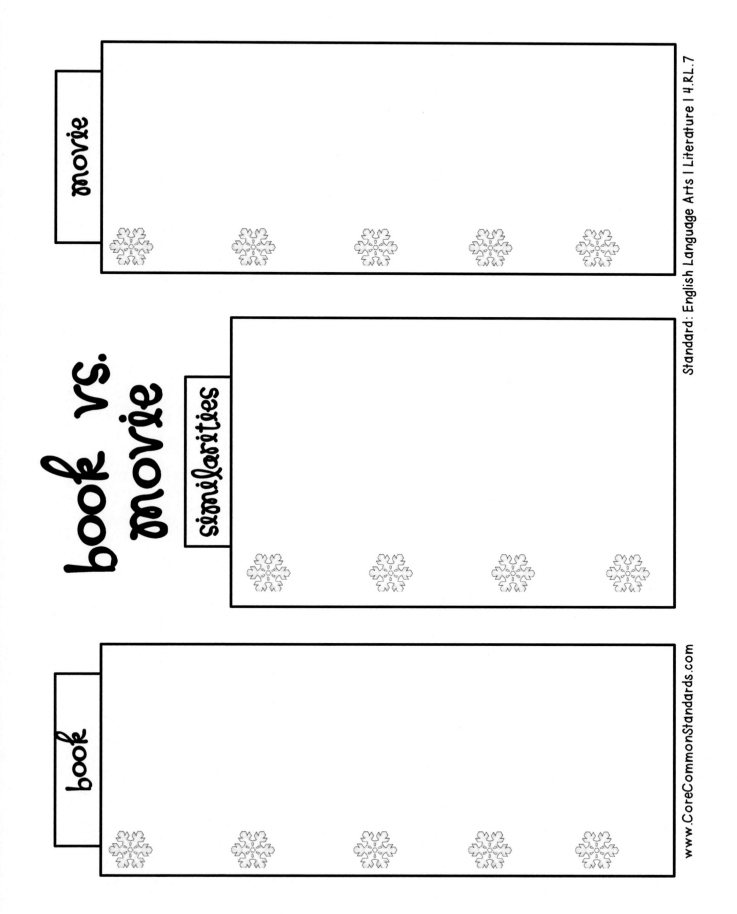

movie

book vs. movie

similarities

book

Standard: English Language Arts | Literature | 4.RL.7

www.CoreCommonStandards.com

This is a Blank Page

You May Cut Out Resources On Back

This is a Blank Page

Compare and Contrast Across Cultures

Directions

Use the Venn Diagram to compare and contrast themes and topics and patterns of events in stories, myths, and traditional literature from different cultures.

Standard: English Language Arts I Reading Literature I RL.4.9

www.CoreCommonStandards.com

This is a Blank Page

You May Cut Out Resources On Back

This is a Blank Page

The Story of Anansi the Spider

Anansi the spider was greedy. One day, Turtle came to visit as Anansi was about to eat his dinner.

"What a nice dinner!" said Turtle. To be polite, Anansi had to offer to share the food. Still, he did not want to.

"You can join me," said Anansi. "But first, clean your hands." Turtle's hands were dirty. He went to the river and washed. When he came back, Anansi had started to eat.

"Your hands are still dirty!" Anansi said.

Turtle looked down. On his way back, he had walked through mud. So he went and washed again. When he returned, he found that Anansi had eaten all the food.

"Tomorrow you must come to my house to share my dinner," said Turtle. The next day, a hungry Anansi met Turtle at the river. Turtle dove into the water to his home on the river bottom. Anansi jumped into the water and tried to swim down, but he was too light. Then, Anansi put stones in his pockets and sank down to Turtle's home. Turtle had started to eat. Turtle looked at Anansi and said, "It is not polite to eat with your coat on. You must take it off." Anansi took off his coat. Without the stones, he was light again. He floated up to the surface. From there, he watched Turtle finish his meal.

www.CoreCommonStandards.com   Standard: English Language Arts I Reading Literature I RL.4.9

This is a Blank Page

You May Cut Out Resources On Back

This is a Blank Page

The Tale of Coyote and Hen

One day, Coyote came upon Hen. She was sitting on a tree branch. Coyote was hungry. He decided that he would eat Hen. But how could he reach her? She was much too high in the tree. Coyote thought and thought. Then he had an idea.

"Oh, Hen," he sighed. "I am so happy! I bring great news." She was interested, but she did not trust Coyote. "A treaty has been signed," said Coyote. "All the animals have signed it. It says that we are all friends now. There will be no more fighting! Please come down from the tree. I am so happy. I would like to give you a big hug."

"Ah," thought Hen. Now she knew what Coyote was up to.

"I would love to," said Hen. "But I see that someone else is coming."

"Really?" asked Coyote. "Who is it?"

"It is Dog," said Hen. Coyote began to shake. Dog scared him.

"He must have heard the news, too," said Hen. "He looks so happy! His eyes are bright and he is so fast. I think he wants to hug you." Coyote took off running as fast as he could. Up in the tree, Hen smiled.

www.CoreCommonStandards.com   Standard: English Language Arts | Reading Literature | RL.4.9

This is a Blank Page

You May Cut Out Resources On Back

This is a Blank Page

Venn Diagram

Use the Venn Diagram to compare and contrast the two books.

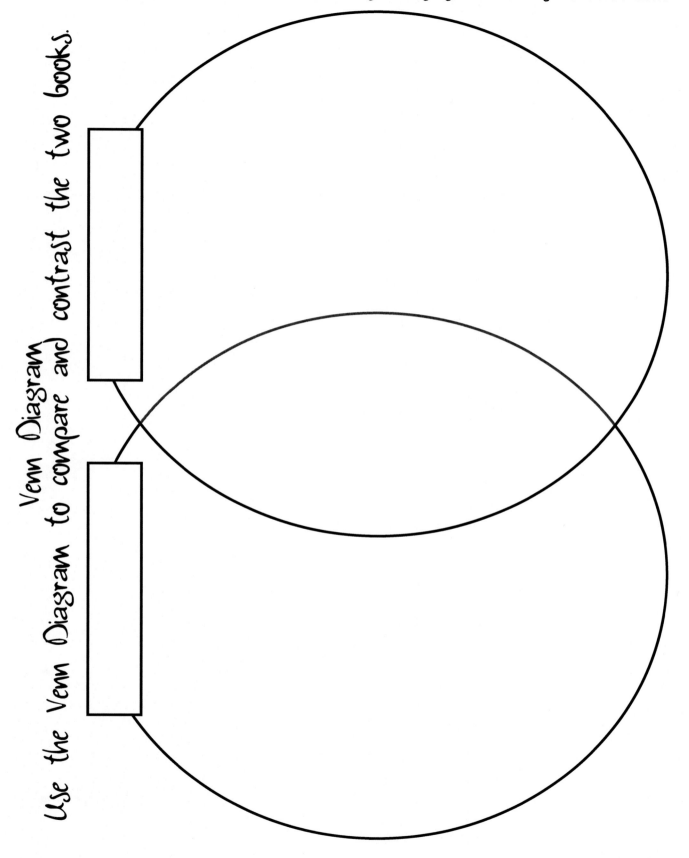

This is a Blank Page

You May Cut Out Resources On Back

This is a Blank Page

Thinking Maps for Reading Journeys

Graphic organizers for reading comprehension

Directions: Respond to the text using graphic organizers.

Standard: By the end of the year, read and comprehend literature, including stories, dramas, and poetry, in the grades 4–5 text complexity band proficiently, with scaffolding as needed at the high end of the range.

Standard: English Language Arts | Reading: Literature | RL.4.10

www.CoreCommonStandards.com

This is a Blank Page

You May Cut Out Resources On Back

This is a Blank Page

Name

Title:
Author:

Text	My Prediction	Outcome

Standard: English Language Arts | Reading: Literature | RL.4.10

www.CoreCommonStandards.com

This is a Blank Page

You May Cut Out Resources On Back

This is a Blank Page

Name _____

Title:		
Author:		
Genre:		

What I saw:

What I read:

www.CoreCommonStandards.com

Standard: English Language Arts | Reading: Literature | RL.4.10

This is a Blank Page

You May Cut Out Resources On Back

This is a Blank Page

Name_____

Title:_____
Author:_____

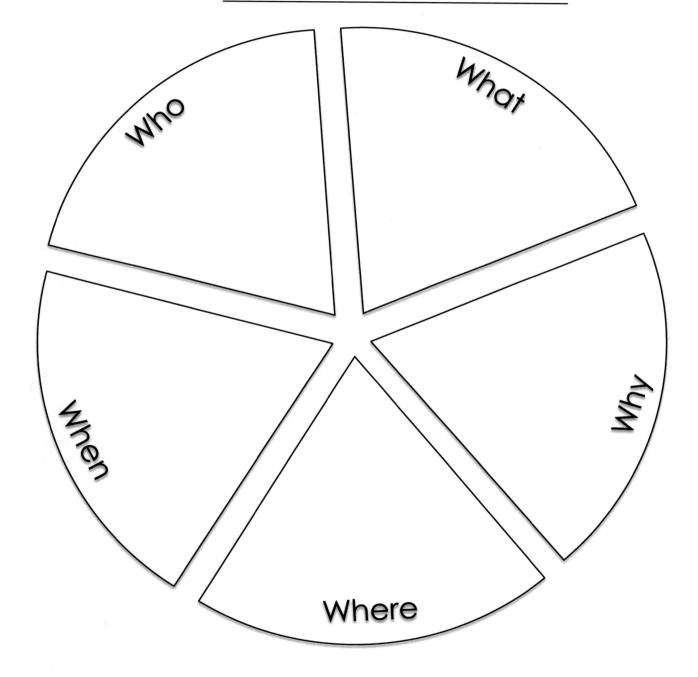

This is a Blank Page

You May Cut Out Resources On Back

This is a Blank Page

Name_____

Title:_____

Author:_____

Main Idea:

Detail:

Detail:

Detail:

This is a Blank Page

You May Cut Out Resources On Back

This is a Blank Page

Name_____

Title:_____

Author:_____

Character(s)

Someone...

Desire/goal

Wanted...

Problem

But...

Solution

So...

This is a Blank Page

You May Cut Out Resources On Back

This is a Blank Page

Name_____

Title:_____
Author:_____

What I read:	My connection:
_____ _____ _____ _____	_____ _____ (circle one) Text-to-Self Text-to-Text Text-to-World
What I read: _____ _____ _____ _____	My connection: _____ _____ (circle one) Text-to-Self Text-to-Text Text-to-World
What I read: _____ _____ _____ _____	My connection: _____ _____ (circle one) Text-to-Self Text-to-Text Text-to-World

Standard: English Language Arts | Reading: Literature | RL.4.10   www.CoreCommonStandards.com

This is a Blank Page

You May Cut Out Resources On Back

This is a Blank Page

Hurricanes

Standard: Refer to details and examples in a text when explaining what the text says explicitly and when drawing inferences from the text.

Directions: Match the vocabulary cards to the correct definitions. Read the passage "Hurricanes" and refer to the text to complete the activity sheet.

Standard: English Language Arts | Reading | RI.4.1

www.CoreCommonStandards.com

This is a Blank Page

You May Cut Out Resources On Back

This is a Blank Page

I can explain what the text says by referring to details and examples in the text.

text

refer

This is a Blank Page

You May Cut Out Resources On Back

This is a Blank Page

The actual wording of anything written or printed, words

To draw a conclusion; Figure out or understand

To seek or look for information

infer

This is a Blank Page

You May Cut Out Resources On Back

This is a Blank Page

Hurricanes

1.   Hurricanes are large tropical storms that develop in the oceans of the world, typically near the continent of Africa. Hurricanes gather heat and energy from the warm ocean water. The heat from these warm currents increase the power of the hurricane. Hurricanes weaken once they get over land, but can become stronger the longer they stay over the warm ocean waters.

2.   Hurricanes are given names, and a new list of names is created each year. The first hurricane name starts with the letter A, like Austin, and the names move through the alphabet as more hurricanes form. Hurricane clouds move in a circle around a point called the eye, which is the center of the storm. To be classified as a hurricane, the storm must have wind speeds of at least 74 miles per hour. When a hurricane comes ashore, there are heavy rains, large waves, and strong winds that cause damage to buildings, cars, and trees. Flooding can occur when large waves called storm surges hit the beaches. Storm surges are the main reason people are told to leave beach towns or to evacuate when a hurricane approaches. Hurricanes move very slowly, so people have a chance to get out of the way.

3.   During the official hurricane season, which lasts from June 1 to November 30, the large storms sometimes hit coastal areas of the United States. As these hurricanes approach, there is rain and strong winds. Meteorologists, scientists who study the weather, watch these storms very carefully. They classify hurricanes into five categories depending upon how strong the hurricane's winds are. Category 1 and 2 hurricanes are the weakest hurricanes, Category 3 storms are in the middle, and Category 4 and 5 hurricanes are the strongest. In recent years, the United States has been hit by more damaging hurricanes than ever before.

This is a Blank Page

You May Cut Out Resources On Back

This is a Blank Page

Name _____

Date _____

Hurricanes

Directions: Refer to the text to answer the questions. Provide the paragraph number for the location of each answer.

1. Which category of hurricane would cause the least damage?

    A. Category 1
    B. Category 2
    C. Category 3
    D. Category 4

Paragraph _____

2. Why would people who live on the coast or islands have time to evacuate?

    A. Storm surges do not cause much damage.
    B. Hurricanes move slowly.
    C. Hurricanes weaken over land.
    D. Wind gusts cause little damage.

Paragraph _____

3. Kylie is the 11th hurricane to hit the U.S.A this season. What might be the name of the next hurricane?

    A. George
    B. Sarah
    C. Jill
    D. Lisa

Paragraph _____

4. When might you expect a hurricane to strike the United States?

    A. December
    B. August
    C. February
    D. May

Paragraph _____

5. What could you infer about a storm with winds of 61 mph?

    A. It is a Category 4
    B. It is a Category 1
    C. It would be a very strong storm.
    D. It would not be classified as a hurricane.

Paragraph _____

Match:

6. _____ infer   a. to seek or look for information

7. _____ text   b. to draw a conclusion; figure out or understand

8. _____ refer   c. the actual wording of anything written or printed, words.

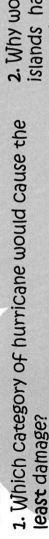

This is a Blank Page

You May Cut Out Resources On Back

This is a Blank Page

What's the Main Idea?

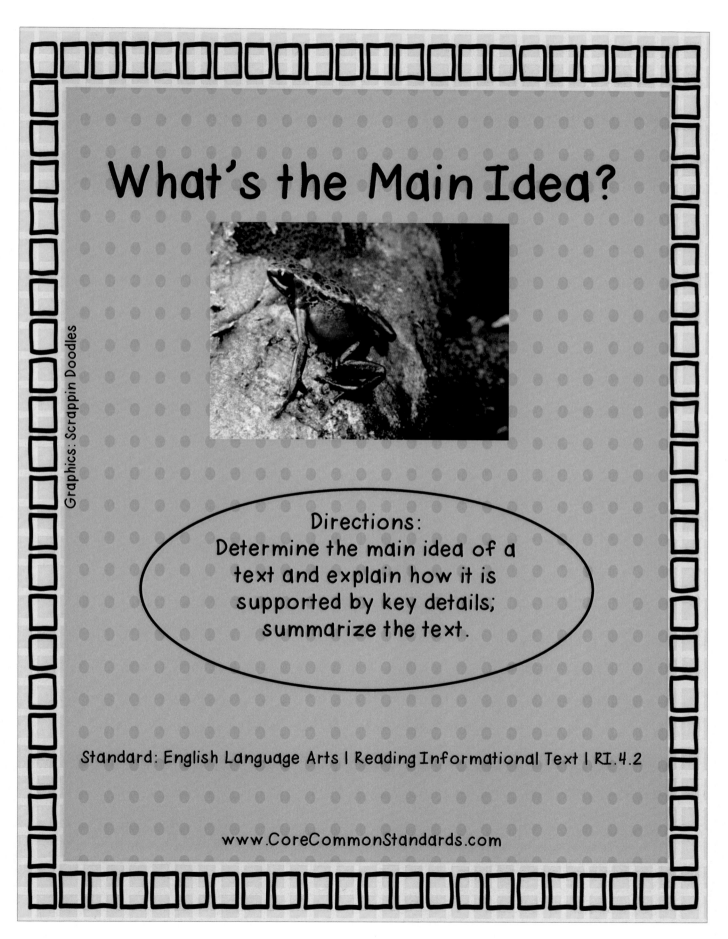

Directions:
Determine the main idea of a text and explain how it is supported by key details; summarize the text.

Standard: English Language Arts | Reading Informational Text | RI.4.2

www.CoreCommonStandards.com

This is a Blank Page

You May Cut Out Resources On Back

This is a Blank Page

The Poison Dart Frog
By: National Geographic (Adapted by Have Fun Teaching)

Poison dart frogs wear some of the most brilliant and beautiful colors on Earth. Depending on their habitats, which are from the tropical forests of Costa Rica to Brazil, their coloring can be yellow, gold, copper, red, green, blue, or black. Their designs and colors scare off predators.

You may have seen monkeys carrying their children on their backs. Well, some of these frogs show some of these parenting habits, including carrying both eggs and tadpoles on their backs. These frogs are some of the most toxic animals on Earth. The two-inch-long Golden Poison Dart Frog has enough venom to kill 10 grown men. Indigenous people of Colombia have used its powerful venom for centuries to tip their blowgun darts when hunting.

Scientists are not sure why these poison dart frogs are so poisonous, but it is possible they take in plant poisons which are carried by their prey, including ants, termites and beetles. Poison dart frogs raised in captivity and isolated from insects in their native habitat never develop venom.

The medical research community has been exploring ways to use poison dart frog venom in medicine. Scientists have already used their venom to create a painkiller medicine.

This is a Blank Page

You May Cut Out Resources On Back

This is a Blank Page

What's the Main Idea?

Main Idea:

Supporting Detail	Supporting Detail	Supporting Detail

Summary:

_____

_____

_____

_____

This is a Blank Page

You May Cut Out Resources On Back

This is a Blank Page

Why, Oh Why?

Directions

Use the graphic organizer to explain events and why they happened, using evidence from the text.

Standard: English Language Arts | Informational | RI 4.3

www.CoreCommonStandards.com

Graphics: Scrappin Doodles

This is a Blank Page

You May Cut Out Resources On Back

This is a Blank Page

A New Car

Story from HaveFunTeaching.com

Larry's dad had a car that was 10 years old. His dad loved his car. It was black and had over 80,000 miles. Larry's dad said that it was time to get a new car, but he wasn't sure if the new cars would be as reliable as his car of 10 years. "Dad," said Larry. "You need to get a new car." "You don't want to have a car that is really old." Larry's dad knew he needed to get a new car, but the problem was he just didn't have enough money right now to buy a new car. Deep down, Larry knew that his dad was having money problems. Larry decided to take the money he had saved over the last two years from birthdays, Christmas, his bank account, and his allowance and give it to his dad to help buy the new car.

Larry left for school the next morning, but not before he left an envelope by his dad's plate at the table. In the envelope there was $1,000. Larry's dad came into the kitchen to eat breakfast and saw the envelope. "What is this?" he asked Larry's mom. "Larry left that envelope before he went for school," said mom. Larry's dad opened the envelope and saw the $1,000 that Larry had given his dad for the new car. "There's a $1,000 in here!" exclaimed Larry's dad. Larry's mom said, "Larry wanted to help you with the payment for the new car."

That afternoon, Larry's dad went to the car dealer and got a car that was only one year old. It was a bright red, Larry's favorite color. The money Larry left for him was enough to pay for the new car. Larry's dad even had some money left over. With the money he had left, he bought a surprise gift for Larry.

That night Larry came home and saw the new car in the driveway. "Wow," said Larry. "That is a great car!" "Thanks to you, we got that great car," said Larry's dad. "Thank you so much for being such a generous and caring son." "There is a small gift for you too," said Larry's dad. Larry was so excited to find a new baseball in the box with the bow. Larry loved baseball, and his dad wanted to show how much he appreciated what Larry had done. "Not only do we have a great new car, I got a great new baseball too," said Larry. "Everyone is happy, and that makes me happy too," said Larry.

www.CoreCommonStandards.com   Standard: English Language Arts | Informational | RI.4.3

This is a Blank Page

You May Cut Out Resources On Back

This is a Blank Page

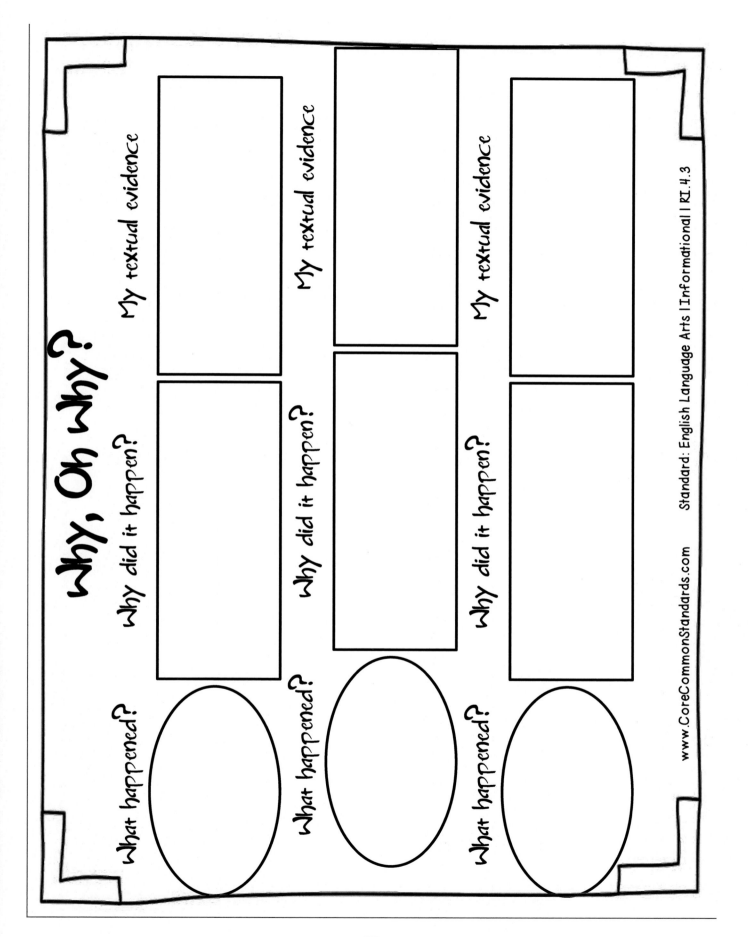

Why, Oh Why?

What happened?

Why did it happen?

My textual evidence

What happened?

Why did it happen?

My textual evidence

What happened?

Why did it happen?

My textual evidence

www.CoreCommonStandards.com

Standard: English Language Arts | Informational | RI.4.3

This is a Blank Page

You May Cut Out Resources On Back

This is a Blank Page

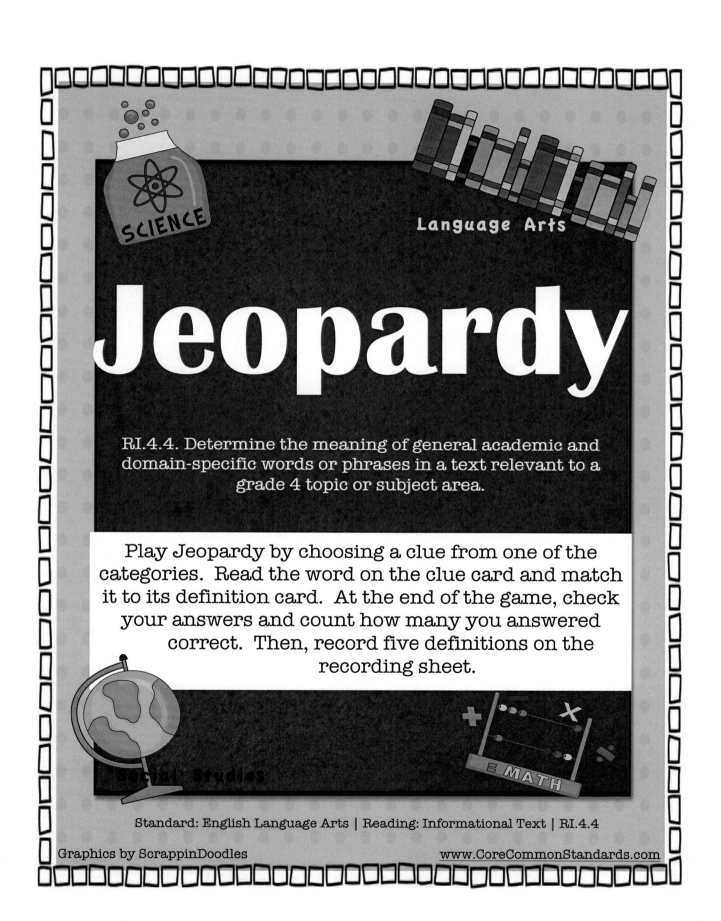

Jeopardy

SCIENCE

Language Arts

RI.4.4. Determine the meaning of general academic and domain-specific words or phrases in a text relevant to a grade 4 topic or subject area.

Play Jeopardy by choosing a clue from one of the categories. Read the word on the clue card and match it to its definition card. At the end of the game, check your answers and count how many you answered correct. Then, record five definitions on the recording sheet.

Social Studies

MATH

Standard: English Language Arts | Reading: Informational Text | RI.4.4

Graphics by ScrappinDoodles

www.CoreCommonStandards.com

This is a Blank Page

You May Cut Out Resources On Back

This is a Blank Page

Category 1	Category 2	Category 3

This is a Blank Page

You May Cut Out Resources On Back

This is a Blank Page

Category 4	Category 5	Category 6

This is a Blank Page

You May Cut Out Resources On Back

This is a Blank Page

Category 7	Category 8	Category 9

This is a Blank Page

You May Cut Out Resources On Back

This is a Blank Page

Plants

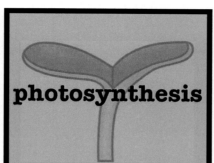

photosynthesis

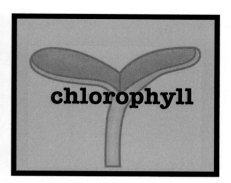

chlorophyll

seed dispersal

decay

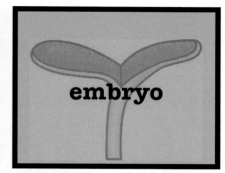

embryo

The scattering or carrying away of seeds from the plant that produced them

The process plants use to make food

A material in plants that traps energy from sunlight and gives leaves green color

To break down into simpler materials

A plant or animal in the earliest stages of development

This is a Blank Page

You May Cut Out Resources On Back

This is a Blank Page

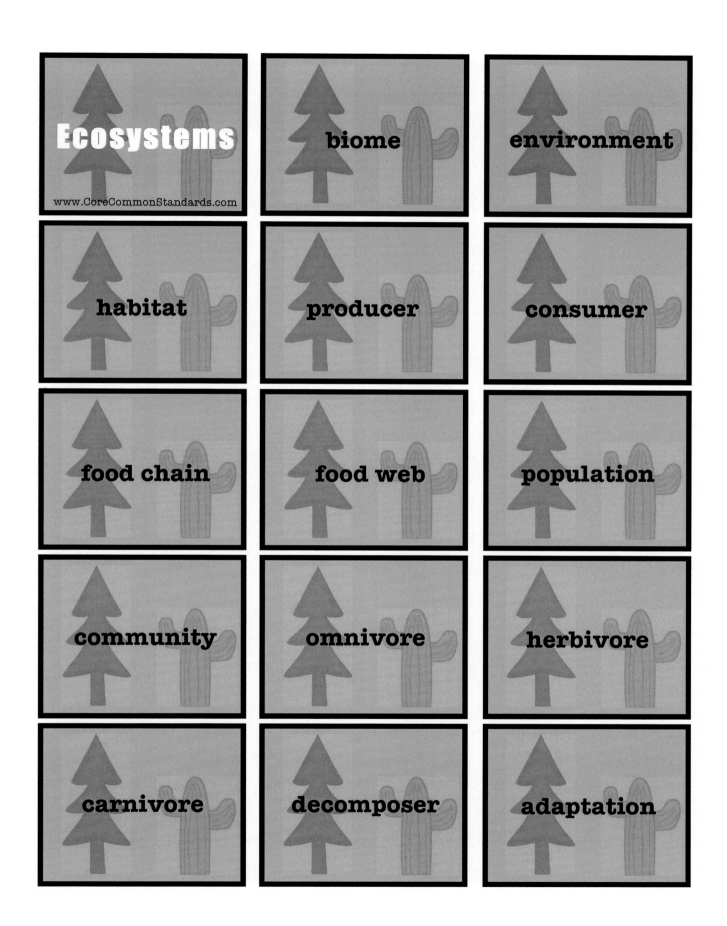

Ecosystems
www.CoreCommonStandards.com

biome

environment

habitat

producer

consumer

food chain

food web

population

community

omnivore

herbivore

carnivore

decomposer

adaptation

This is a Blank Page

You May Cut Out Resources On Back

This is a Blank Page

Ecosystems

Large areas classified by the type of plants and animals living there, the climate, and the soil

Everything that surrounds and affects a living thing

The place where an organism lives

An organism that gets its energy by making it for themselves

An organism that gets its energy by eating other organisms

The path of food energy in an ecosystem when one living thing eats another

Two or more food chains that overlap

A group of the same kind of plant or animal living in an ecosystem

All groups of plants and animals living in the same ecosystem

A consumer that eats both plants and animals

A consumer that only eats plants

A consumer that only eats meat

An organism that breaks down the remains of dead organisms

A body part or behavior that helps something live

This is a Blank Page

You May Cut Out Resources On Back

This is a Blank Page

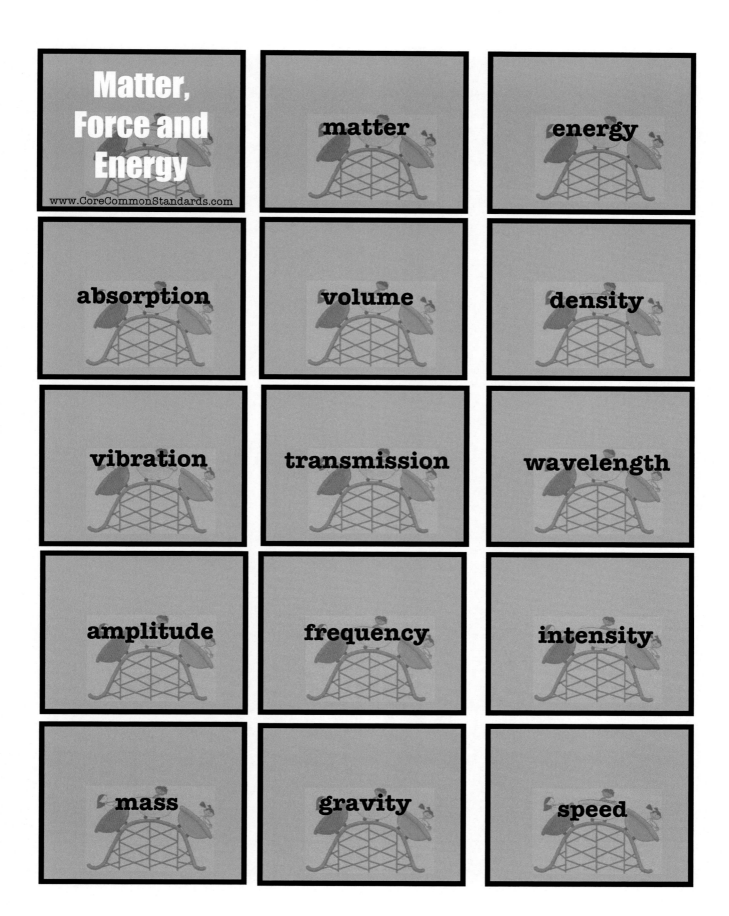

This is a Blank Page

You May Cut Out Resources On Back

This is a Blank Page

Matter, Force and Energy

www.CoreCommonStandards.com

Anything that takes up space and has mass. Refers to any solid, liquid, or gas

The ability to do work

The taking in of light or sound energy by an object

The amount of space an object takes up

The mass of one unit of volume

A quick back and forth motion

Heating through the direct contact of materials

The distance between a point on one wave and the identical point on the next wave

The height of a wave

The number of waves that pass in a second

A measure of how high or low a sound is

The amount of matter an object has

The force of attraction between two objects

The distance traveled over time

This is a Blank Page

You May Cut Out Resources On Back

This is a Blank Page

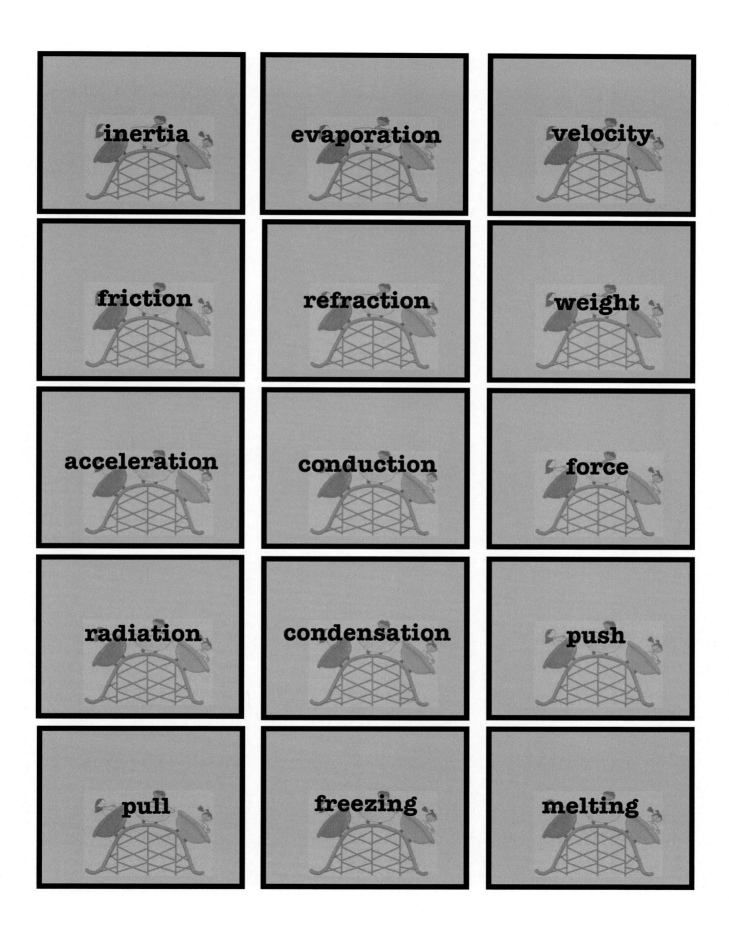

inertia

evaporation

velocity

friction

refraction

weight

acceleration

conduction

force

radiation

condensation

push

pull

freezing

melting

This is a Blank Page

You May Cut Out Resources On Back

This is a Blank Page

The property of matter that keeps an object at rest or moving in a straight line	When a liquid changes to a gas	Both the speed and direction of an object
A force that slows the motion of moving objects	The bending of light	The gravitational force acting on an object
An increase in speed in a given direction	The movement of heat from a warmer area to a cooler area	Causes an object to change speed or direction
Energy that travels through an object	When a gas changes to a liquid	The act of applying force to move an object away
The act of applying force to move an object toward you	When a liquid changes to a solid in cold temperatures	When a solid changes to a liquid

This is a Blank Page

You May Cut Out Resources On Back

This is a Blank Page

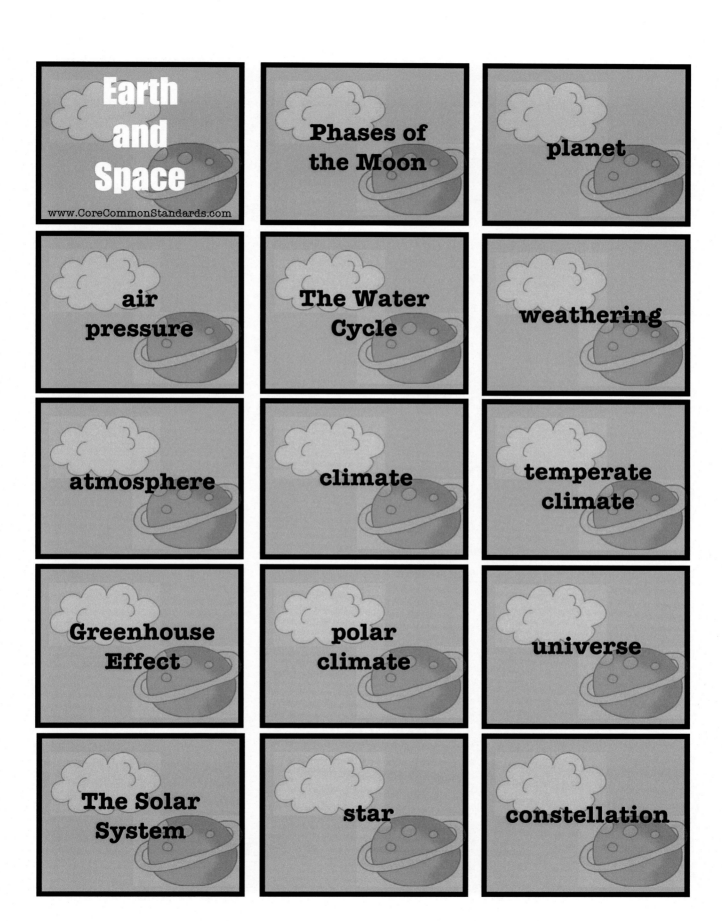

Earth
and
Space

www.CoreCommonStandards.com

Phases of the Moon

planet

air pressure

The Water Cycle

weathering

atmosphere

climate

temperate climate

Greenhouse Effect

polar climate

universe

The Solar System

star

constellation

This is a Blank Page

You May Cut Out Resources On Back

This is a Blank Page

Earth and Space

www.CoreCommonStandards.com

Changes in the amount of sunlight that reaches the side of the Moon that faces Earth

A celestial body orbiting the Sun

The weight of air as it presses down on Earth's surface

The movement of water into the air as water vapor and back to Earth as precipitation

The slow wearing away of rock into smaller pieces

The layers of air that surround Earth's surface

The average weather conditions in an area over a long period of time

Place that usually has warm, dry summers and cold, wet winters

The process by which heat from the Sun builds up near Earth's surface and is trapped by the atmosphere

Place with very cold temperatures all year

The system made up of all the matter and energy; galaxies, stars, planets, and moons

A system made up of the Sun, planets and smaller bodies that orbit the Sun

A huge ball of very hot gasses that gives off light heat and energy

A group of stars that forms a pattern in the night sky

This is a Blank Page

You May Cut Out Resources On Back

This is a Blank Page

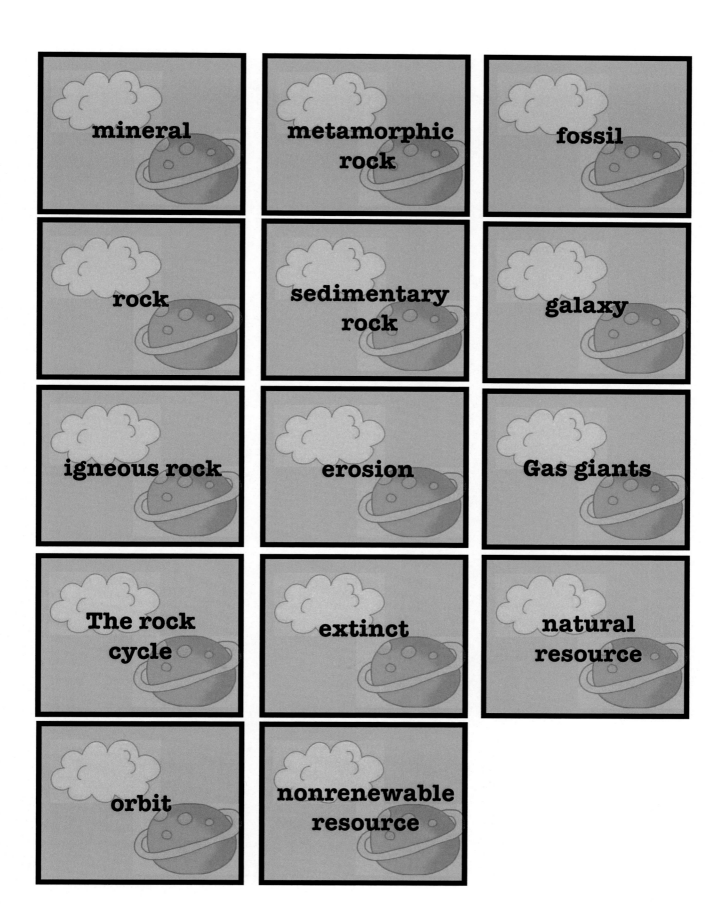

mineral

metamorphic rock

fossil

rock

sedimentary rock

galaxy

igneous rock

erosion

Gas giants

The rock cycle

extinct

natural resource

orbit

nonrenewable resource

This is a Blank Page

You May Cut Out Resources On Back

This is a Blank Page

A solid, nonliving material of specific chemical makeup

When a rock is changed by pressure into a new rock

The preserved traces and remains of an organism that lived long ago

A solid material that is made up of one or more minerals

A type of rock that forms when sediment becomes pressed together and hardens

A huge system or group of stars held together by

The type of rock that is formed when melted rock from inside Earth cools and hardens

The movement of rock material from one place to another

The four largest planets in Earth's solar system: Jupiter, Saturn, Uranus, Neptune

The continuous series of changes that rocks go through

No longer living

A material on Earth that is useful to people

The path that Earth and other planets make moving around the Sun

A resource that can not be replaced once it is used up

This is a Blank Page

You May Cut Out Resources On Back

This is a Blank Page

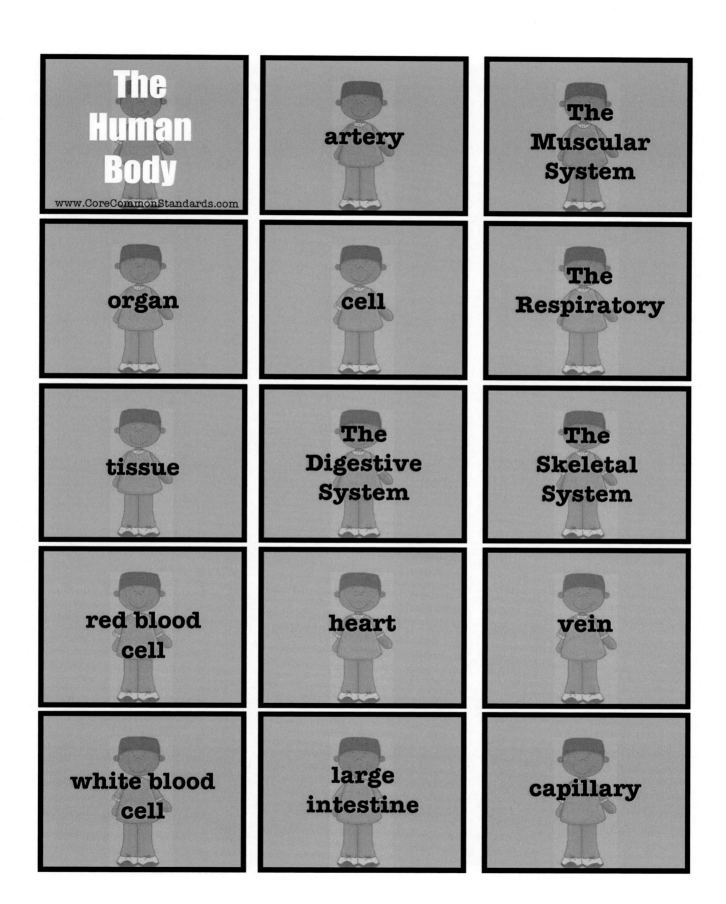

The Human Body

www.CoreCommonStandards.com

artery

The Muscular System

organ

cell

The Respiratory

tissue

The Digestive System

The Skeletal System

red blood cell

heart

vein

white blood cell

large intestine

capillary

This is a Blank Page

You May Cut Out Resources On Back

This is a Blank Page

The Human Body

Any blood vessel that carries blood away from the heart to capillaries

A system made up of muscles and tissues that make body parts move

A special part of an organism's body that performs a specific function

The basic unit that makes up all living things

A group of organs that work together to take air into the body and push it back out

A group of similar cells that work together

Major organ system that processes the food the body takes in

System made up of bones that protect and give the body shape

Cell that delivers oxygen

A muscular pump inside the body that pushes the blood through the blood vessels

Any blood vessel that carries blood back to the heart

Cell that defends the body from sickness

The organ where water and minerals are removed and absorbed into the blood

A tiny blood vessel that connects arteries and veins

This is a Blank Page

You May Cut Out Resources On Back

This is a Blank Page

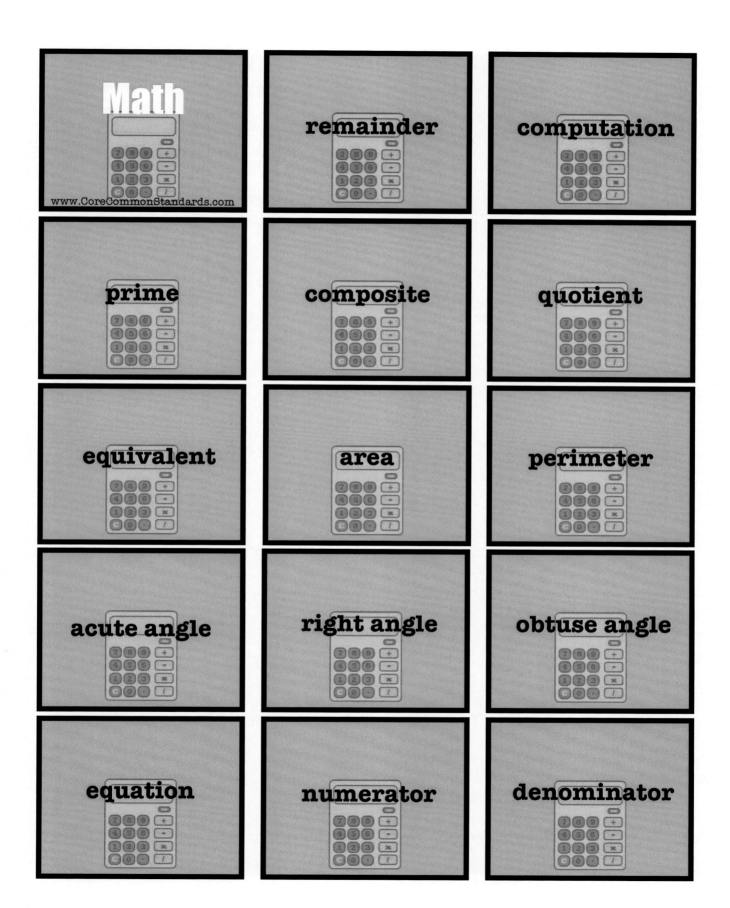

Math

www.CoreCommonStandards.com

remainder

computation

prime

composite

quotient

equivalent

area

perimeter

acute angle

right angle

obtuse angle

equation

numerator

denominator

This is a Blank Page

You May Cut Out Resources On Back

This is a Blank Page

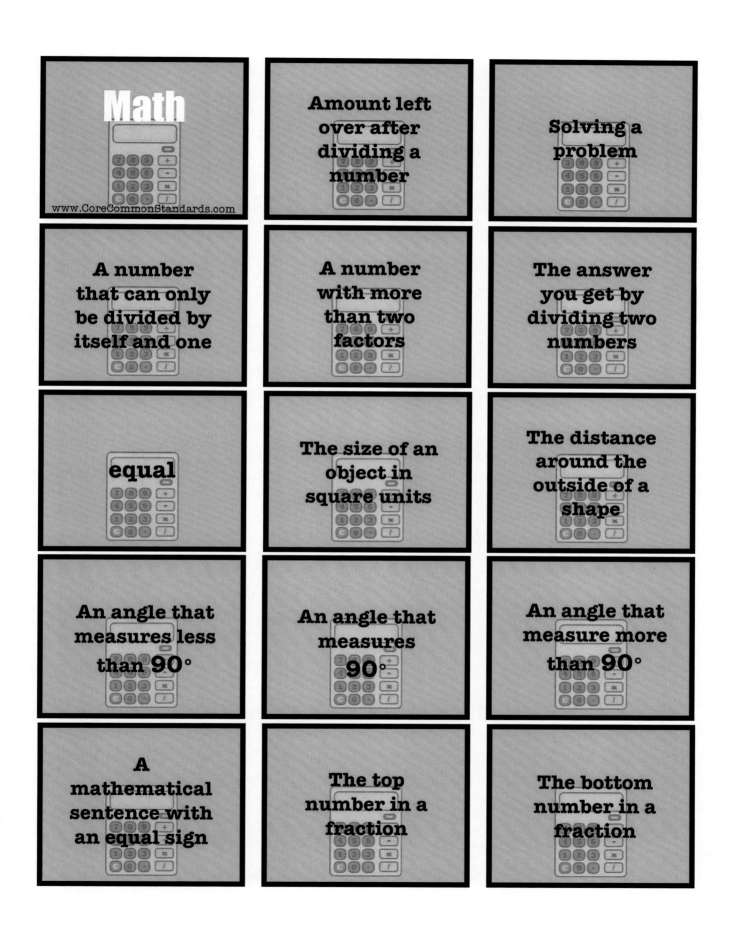

Math

Amount left over after dividing a number

Solving a problem

A number that can only be divided by itself and one

A number with more than two factors

The answer you get by dividing two numbers

equal

The size of an object in square units

The distance around the outside of a shape

An angle that measures less than 90°

An angle that measures 90°

An angle that measure more than 90°

A mathematical sentence with an equal sign

The top number in a fraction

The bottom number in a fraction

This is a Blank Page

You May Cut Out Resources On Back

This is a Blank Page

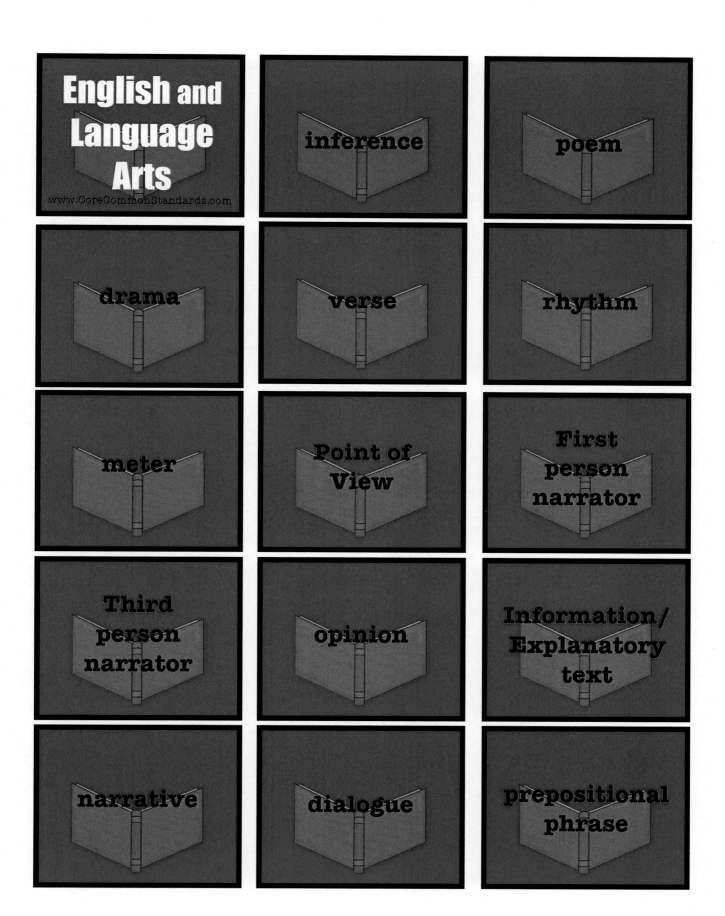

English and Language Arts
www.CoreCommonStandards.com

inference

poem

drama

verse

rhythm

meter

Point of View

First person narrator

Third person narrator

opinion

Information/ Explanatory text

narrative

dialogue

prepositional phrase

This is a Blank Page

You May Cut Out Resources On Back

This is a Blank Page

English and Language Arts

www.CoreCommonStandards.com

Using information to come to a logical conclusion

Writing form that uses language to evoke emotion

Fiction represented in performance

A line in a poem

The pattern of sounds in a poem

The structure of a verse

The perspective of the narrator

The narrator is a character who is talking about himself; uses "I"

The narrator is not a character; uses "he" "she" "they"

A person's beliefs

A text written to give information

A written series of events

A conversation between characters

A phrase describing the location of a subject

This is a Blank Page

You May Cut Out Resources On Back

This is a Blank Page

pronoun	simile	metaphor
idiom	antonym	synonym
A word that substitutes for a noun	A figure of speech comparing two different things using "like" or "as"	A figure of speech in which an expression is used to refer to something that it does not literally mean in order to suggest similarity.
A phrase with a figurative meaning; not literal	Two words that mean the opposite	Two words that mean the same

This is a Blank Page

You May Cut Out Resources On Back

This is a Blank Page

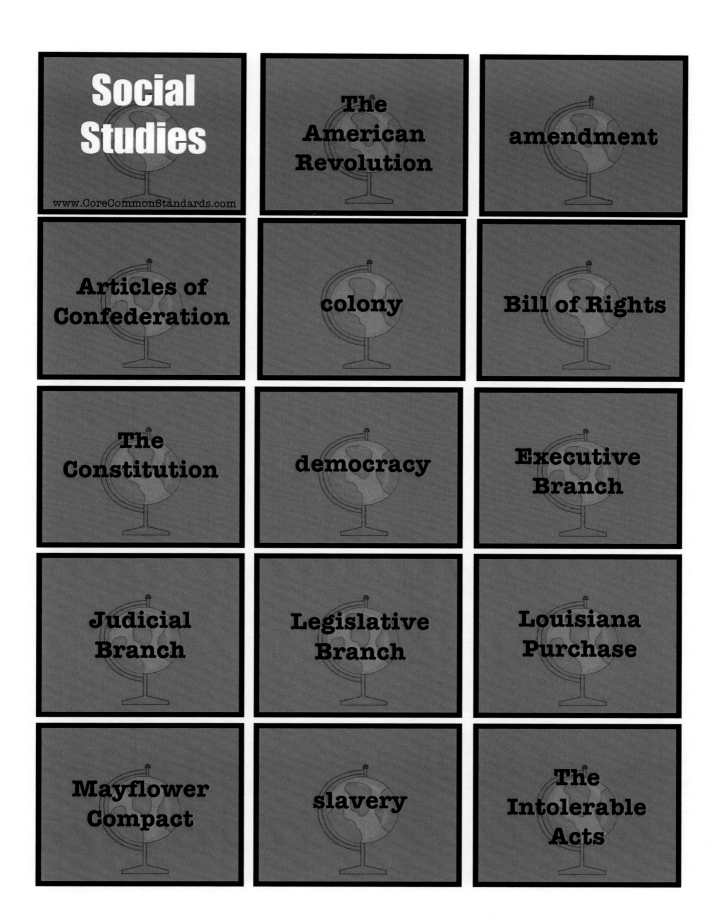

Social Studies

www.CoreCommonStandards.com

The American Revolution

amendment

Articles of Confederation

colony

Bill of Rights

The Constitution

democracy

Executive Branch

Judicial Branch

Legislative Branch

Louisiana Purchase

Mayflower Compact

slavery

The Intolerable Acts

This is a Blank Page

You May Cut Out Resources On Back

This is a Blank Page

Social Studies

The colonies fighting against the British for independence

A change made to the Constitution

The first Constitution ratified by the 13 founding states

A territory ruled by a different country
Ex. American colonies governed by Britain

The first 10 amendments of the Constitution that protect the rights of citizens

The supreme law of the United States

A form of government where all citizens have equal say

The branch that is headed by the President and controls the law

The branch of government made up of the courts that interpret the law

The branch that is headed by Congress to make the laws

Territory purchased from France during Thomas Jefferson's presidency

The first government document of Plymouth Colony

A system where people are bought, sold, and forced to work

A series of laws passed by the British parliament on the colonies

This is a Blank Page

You May Cut Out Resources On Back

This is a Blank Page

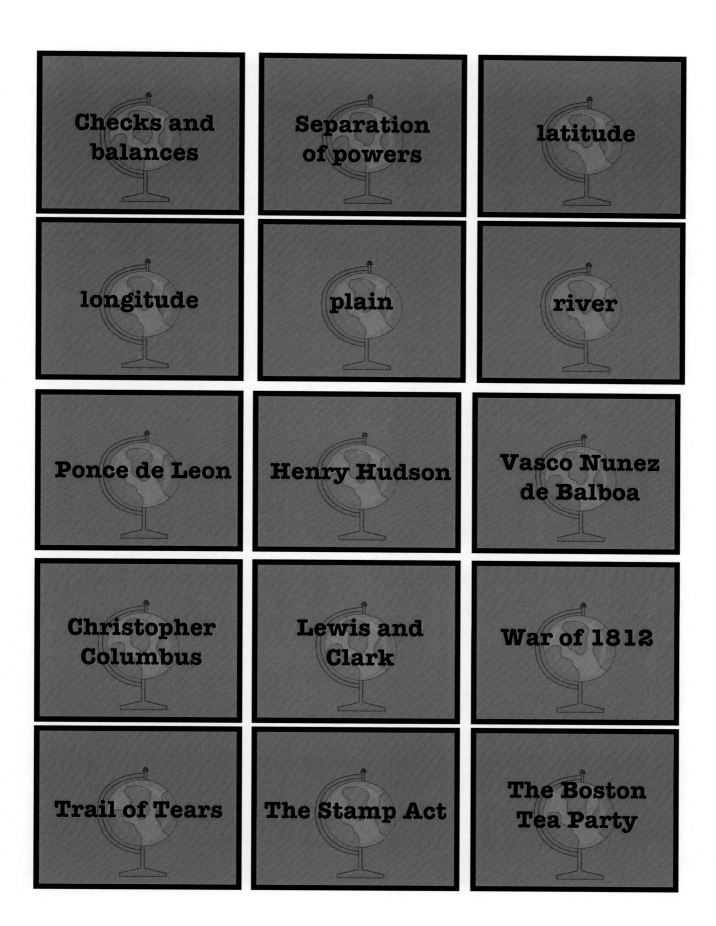

Checks and balances

Separation of powers

latitude

longitude

plain

river

Ponce de Leon

Henry Hudson

Vasco Nunez de Balboa

Christopher Columbus

Lewis and Clark

War of 1812

Trail of Tears

The Stamp Act

The Boston Tea Party

This is a Blank Page

You May Cut Out Resources On Back

This is a Blank Page

Makes sure that one branch of government is not too powerful	The dividing of government into three branches with their own powers	Lines run north to south and help pinpoint locations on the Earth's surface
Lines run east to west and help pinpoint locations on the Earth's surface	A mostly flat area of land	A flowing body of water
A Spanish explorer who discovered Florida	Explored many waterways in the	Spanish explorer that crossed the Isthmus of Panama to the Pacific Ocean
Italian explorer that sailed in 1492	Exploration of the Western half of the United States	War between America and Britain
The forced relocation of Native Americans	Tax of all paper goods on American colonies	A political protest against the British government

This is a Blank Page

You May Cut Out Resources On Back

This is a Blank Page

Name _____

Directions: Write down **five** words and their definitions from your Jeopardy cards.

Word	Definition

Standard: English Language Arts | Reading: Informational Text | RI.4.4
Graphics by ScrappinDoodles   www.CoreCommonStandards.com

This is a Blank Page

You May Cut Out Resources On Back

This is a Blank Page

Word and Definition Answer Sheet

Plants

Chlorophyll	A material in plants that traps energy from sunlight and gives leaves green color
Decay	To break down into simpler materials
Embryo	A plant or animal in the earliest stages of development
Photosynthesis	The process plants use to make food
Seed dispersal	The scattering or carrying away of seeds from the plant that produced them

Ecosystems

Adaptation	A body part or behavior that helps something live
Biome	Large areas classified by the type of plants and animals living there, the climate and the soil.
Carnivore	A consumer that only eats meat
Community	All groups of plants and animals living in the same ecosystem
Consumer	An organism that gets its energy by eating other organisms
Decomposer	An organism that breaks down the remains of dead organisms
Environment	Everything that surrounds and affects a living thing.
Food chain	The path of food energy in an ecosystem when one living thing eats another
Food web	Two or more food chains that overlap
Habitat	The place where an organism lives
Herbivore	A consumer that only eats plants
Omnivore	A consumer that eats both plants and animals
Population	A group of the same kind of plant or animal living in an ecosystem
Producer	An organism that gets its energy by making it for themselves

This is a Blank Page

You May Cut Out Resources On Back

This is a Blank Page

Matter, Force and Energy

Absorption	The taking in of light or sound energy by an object
Acceleration	An increase in speed in a given direction
Amplitude	The height of a wave
Condensation	When a gas changes to a liquid
Conduction	The movement of heat from a warmer area to a cooler area
Density	The mass of one unit of volume
Energy	The ability to do work
Evaporation	When a liquid changes to a gas
Frequency	The number of waves that pass in a second
Force	Causes an object to change speed or direction
Freezing	When a liquid changes to a solid in cold temperatures
Friction	A force that slows the motion of moving objects

Gravity	The force of attraction between two objects
Inertia	The property of matter that keeps an object at rest or moving in a straight line
Intensity	A measure of how high or low a sound is
Mass	The amount of matter an object has
Matter	Anything that takes up space and has mass. Refers to any solid, liquid, or gas
Melting	When a solid changes to a liquid
Pull	The act of applying force to move an object toward you
Push	The act of applying force to move an object away
Radiation	Energy that travels through an object
Refraction	The bending of light

Speed	The distance traveled over time
Transmission	Heating through the direct contact of materials
Vibration	A quick back and forth motion
Velocity	Both the speed and direction of an object
Volume	The amount of space an object takes up
Wavelength	The distance between a point on one wave and the identical point on the next wave
Weight	The gravitational force acting on an object

This is a Blank Page

You May Cut Out Resources On Back

This is a Blank Page

Earth and Space

Air pressure	The weight of air as it presses down on Earth's surface
Atmosphere	The layers of air that surround Earth's surface
Climate	The average weather conditions in an area over a long period of time
Constellation	A group of stars that forms a pattern in the night sky
Erosion	The movement of rock material from one place to another
Extinct	No longer living
Fossil	The preserved traces and remains of an organism that lived long ago
Galaxy	A huge system or group of stars held together by gravity.
Gas giants	The four largest planets in Earth's solar system. Jupiter, Saturn, Uranus, Neptune
Greenhouse Effect	The process by which heat from the Sun builds up near Earth's surface and is trapped by the atmosphere
Igneous rock	The type of rock that is formed when melted rock from inside Earth cools and hardens
Metamorphic rock	When a rock is changed by pressure into a new rock
Mineral	A solid, nonliving material of specific chemical makeup
Natural resource	A material on Earth that is useful to people
Nonrenewable resource	A resource that can not be replaced once it is used up
Orbit	The path that Earth and other planets make moving around the Sun
Planet	A celestial body orbiting the Sun
Phases of the moon	Changes in the amount of sunlight that reaches the side of the Moon that faces Earth
Polar climate	Place with very cold temperatures all year
Rock	A solid material that is made up of one or more minerals
Sedimentary rock	A type of rock that forms when sediment becomes pressed together and hardens
Star	A huge ball of very hot gasses that gives off light heat and energy
Temperate climate	Place that usually has warm, dry summers and cold, wet winters.
The rock cycle	The continuous series of changes that rocks go through.
The Solar System	A system made up of the Sun, planets and smaller bodies that orbit the Sun.

This is a Blank Page

You May Cut Out Resources On Back

This is a Blank Page

The Water Cycle	The movement of water into the air as water vapor and back to Earth as precipitation
Weathering	The slow wearing away of rock into smaller pieces
Universe	The system made up of all the matter and energy; galaxies, stars, planets, and moons

The Human Body

Artery	Any blood vessel that carries blood away from the heart to capillaries
Cell	The basic unit that makes up all living things
Capillary	A tiny blood vessel that connects arteries and veins
Heart	A muscular pump inside the body that pushes the blood through the blood vessels
Large intestine	The organ where water and minerals are removed and absorbed into the blood
Organ	A special part of an organism's body that performs a specific function
Red blood cell	Cell that delivers oxygen
The Digestive System	Major organ system that processes the food the body takes in
The Muscular System	A system made up of muscles and tissues that make body parts move
The Respiratory System	A group of organs that work together to take air into the body and push it back out
The Skeletal System	System made up of bones that protect and give the body shape
Tissue	A group of similar cells that work together
Vein	Any blood vessel that carries blood back to the heart
White blood cell	Cell that defends the body from sickness

This is a Blank Page

You May Cut Out Resources On Back

This is a Blank Page

Math

Acute angle	An angle that measure less than 90°
Area	The size of an object in square units
Composite	A number with more than two factors
Computation	Solving a problem
Denominator	The bottom number in a fraction
Equation	A mathematical sentence with an equal sign
Equivalent	equal
Numerator	The top number in a fraction
Obtuse angle	An angle that measure more than 90°
Perimeter	The distance around the outside of a shape
Prime	A number that can only be divided by itself and one
Quotient	The answer you get by dividing two numbers
Remainder	Amount left over after dividing a number
Right angle	An angle that measures 90°

This is a Blank Page

You May Cut Out Resources On Back

This is a Blank Page

English Language Arts

Antonym	Two words that mean the opposite
Dialogue	A conversation between characters
Drama	Fiction represented in performance
First Person narrator	The narrator is a character who is talking about himself; uses "I"
Idiom	A phrase with a figurative meaning; not literal
Inference	Using information to come to a logical conclusion
Informational/ Explanatory text	A text written to give information
Metaphor	A figure of speech in which an expression is used to refer something that it does not literally mean in order to suggest a similarity
Meter	The structure of a verse
Narrative	A written series of events
Opinion	A person's beliefs
Poem	Writing form that uses language to evoke emotion
Point of View	The perspective of the narrator
Prepositional phrase	A phrase describing the location of a subject
Pronoun	A word that substitutes for a noun
Rhythm	The pattern of sounds in a poem
Simile	A figure of speech comparing two different things using "like" or "as"
Synonym	Two words that mean the same
Third person narrator	The narrator is not a character; uses "he" "she" "they"
Verse	A line in a poem

This is a Blank Page

You May Cut Out Resources On Back

This is a Blank Page

Social Studies

Amendment	A change made to the Constitution
Articles of Confederation	The first Constitution ratified by the 13 founding states
Bill of Rights	The first 10 amendments of the Constitution that protect the rights of citizens
Colony	A territory ruled by a different country Ex. American colonies governed by Britain
Checks and balances	Makes sure that one branch of government is not too powerful
Christopher Columbus	Italian explorer that sailed in 1492
Democracy	A form of government where all citizens have equal say
Executive branch	The branch that is headed by the President and controls the law
Henry Hudson	Explored many waterways in the Northeast
Judicial branch	The branch of government made up of the courts that interpret the law
Latitude	Lines run north to south and help pinpoint locations on the Earth's surface
Legislative branch	The branch that is headed by Congress to make the laws
Lewis and Clark	Exploration of the Western half of the United States
Longitude	Lines run east to west and help pinpoint locations on the Earth's surface
Louisiana purchase	Territory purchased from France during Thomas Jefferson's presidency
Mayflower compact	The first government document of Plymouth Colony
Plain	A mostly flat area of land
Ponce de Leon	A Spanish explorer who discovered Florida
River	A flowing body of water
Separation of powers	The dividing of government into three branches with their own powers
Slavery	A system where people are bought, sold, and forced to work
The American revolution	The colonies fighting against the British for independence

This is a Blank Page

You May Cut Out Resources On Back

This is a Blank Page

The Boston Tea Party	A political protest against the British government
The Constitution	The supreme law of the United States
The Intolerable Acts	A series of laws passed by the British parliament on the colonies
The Stamp Act	Tax of all paper goods on American colonies
Trail of Tears	The forced relocation of Native Americans
Vasco Nunez de Balboa	Spanish explorer that crossed the Isthmus of Panama to the Pacific Ocean
War of 1812	War between America and Britain

This is a Blank Page

You May Cut Out Resources On Back

This is a Blank Page

Digging for Information

Directions: Use the graphic organizers to arrange the ideas and concepts you gather from informational texts.

Standard: Describe the overall structure (e.g., chronology, comparison, cause/effect, problem/solution) of events, ideas, concepts, or information in a text or part of a text.

Standard: English Language Arts |Reading: Informational Texts | RI.4.5
Graphics by ScrappinDoodles   www.CoreCommonStandards.com

This is a Blank Page

You May Cut Out Resources On Back

This is a Blank Page

Name_____

Title:_____

Author:_____

First:

Next:

Next:

Next:

Next:

Next:

Next:

Last:

This is a Blank Page

You May Cut Out Resources On Back

This is a Blank Page

Name_____

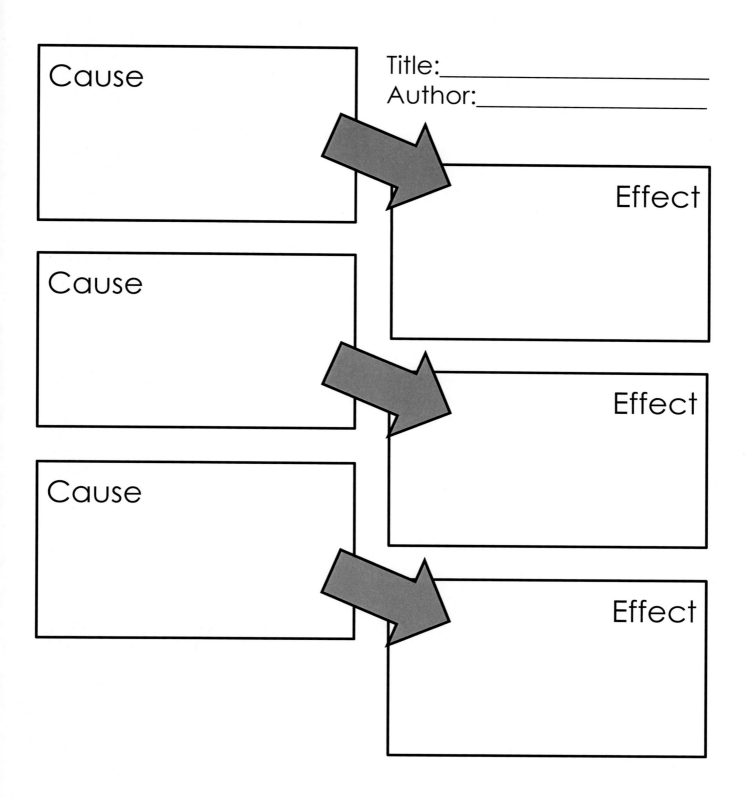

Cause

Title:_____
Author:_____

Effect

Cause

Effect

Cause

Effect

Standard: English Language Arts | Reading: Informational Texts | RI.4.5   www.CoreCommonStandards.com

This is a Blank Page

You May Cut Out Resources On Back

This is a Blank Page

Name _____

Title: _____
Author: _____

Topic: _____

Topic: _____

Different

Alike

Different

Standard: English Language Arts | Reading: Informational Texts | RI.4.5

This is a Blank Page

You May Cut Out Resources On Back

This is a Blank Page

Name _____

Title: _____
Author: _____

Topic: _____

Topic: _____

Contrast

Compare

Contrast

Standard: English Language Arts | Reading: Informational Texts | RI.4.5

This is a Blank Page

You May Cut Out Resources On Back

This is a Blank Page

Name_____

Title:_____

Author:_____

Main Idea:

Detail:

Detail:

Detail:

This is a Blank Page

You May Cut Out Resources On Back

This is a Blank Page

Name_____

Title:_____

Author:_____

Problem:

_____

_____

Possible Solution #1

_____

_____

Pro:

_____

Con:

_____

_____

Possible Solution #2

_____

_____

Pro:

_____

Con:

_____

_____

Possible Solution #3

_____

_____

Pro:

_____

Con:

_____

_____

The Best Solution:

_____

This is a Blank Page

You May Cut Out Resources On Back

This is a Blank Page

Firsthand and Secondhand Accounts

Directions:

Read both accounts of the same event. Using the text, describe the differences in focus and the information provided.

Standard: English Language Arts | Informational | RI.4.6

www.CoreCommonStandards.com

This is a Blank Page

You May Cut Out Resources On Back

This is a Blank Page

Firsthand and Secondhand Accounts

Firsthand Account

Secondhand Account

Similarities between the two accounts

This is a Blank Page

You May Cut Out Resources On Back

This is a Blank Page

Firsthand Account

May 21, 1849
We have a cooking stove made of sheet iron, a portable table, tin plates and cups, cheap knives and forks (best ones packed away), camp stools, etc. We sleep in our wagons on feather beds.... We live on bacon, ham, rice, dried fruits, molasses, packed butter, bread, coffee, tea, and milk, as we have our own cows.

July 2, 1849
Passed Independence Rock. This rock is covered with names. With great difficulty, I found a place to cut mine. Twelve miles from this is Devil's Gate. It's an opening in the mountain through which the Sweetwater River flows. Several of us climbed this mountain—somewhat perilous for youngsters not over fourteen.... We were gone so long that the train was stopped and men sent out in search of us. We made all sorts of promises to remain in sight in the future.

Sallie Hester, 14 years old

Excerpt from: Primary Sources for the Interactive Whiteboard
By: Karen Baicker

www.CoreCommonStandards.com   Standard: English Language Arts | Informational | RI.4.6

This is a Blank Page

You May Cut Out Resources On Back

This is a Blank Page

Secondhand Account

The Oregon Trail

   The Oregon Trail is the most famous of the trails pioneers carved out of the rugged landscape of the West. The trails began at Independence, Missouri and followed the south bank of the Platte River, continued West through Nebraska, into Wyoming, and through the Rocky Mountains all the way to Oregon. The route was over 2,000 miles long.

   Settlers were encouraged to take the trip by offers of free land from the United States government. More than 350,000 people made the arduous trip, one filled with hardship and peril.

   The Pioneer Train Constitution of 1849 was written by the leaders of a wagon trains. Groups often elected leaders to write such rules of conduct during the first weeks on the trail.

Excerpt from: Primary Sources for the Interactive Whiteboard
By: Karen Baicker

www.CoreCommonStandards.com   Standard: English Language Arts | Informational | RI.4.6

This is a Blank Page

You May Cut Out Resources On Back

This is a Blank Page

Graphics: Scrappin Doodles

Contributions to the Text

Directions

Interpret information presented visually, orally, or quantitatively and explain how the information contributes to an understanding of the text in which it appears.

Standard: English Language Arts | Reading Informational Text | RI.4.7

www.CoreCommonStandards.com

This is a Blank Page

You May Cut Out Resources On Back

This is a Blank Page

Visual Information

Sketch	Contribution to Text
Sketch	Contribution to Text
Sketch	Contribution to Text
Sketch	Contribution to Text

This is a Blank Page

You May Cut Out Resources On Back

This is a Blank Page

Orally Presented Information

Quote	Contribution to Text
Quote	Contribution to Text
Quote	Contribution to Text
Quote	Contribution to Text

This is a Blank Page

You May Cut Out Resources On Back

This is a Blank Page

aNIMaL MyTH bUSters

Directions:
Use the animal myth busters to
explain how an author uses reasons
and evidence to support particular
points in a text.

Standards: English Language Arts | Reading Informational | RI.4.8

www.CoreCommonStandards.com

This is a Blank Page

You May Cut Out Resources On Back

This is a Blank Page

Animal Myth Busters
By: Stephen Lovgren

Myth
Touching a frog or toad will give you warts.

How It Started
Many frogs and toads have bumps on their skin that look like warts. Some people think the bumps are contagious.

Why It's Not True
"Warts are caused by a human virus, not frogs or toads," says dermatologist Jerry Litt. But the wartlike bumps behind a toad's ears can be dangerous. These parotoid glands contain a nasty poison that irritates the mouths of some predators and often the skin of humans. So toads may not cause warts, but they can cause other nasties. It's best not to handle these critters - warts and all!

www.CoreCommonStandards.com   Standards: English Language Arts | Reading Informational | RI.4.8

This is a Blank Page

You May Cut Out Resources On Back

This is a Blank Page

Animal Myth Busters
By: Stephen Lovgren

Myth
Ostriches bury their heads in the sand when they're scared or threatened.

How It Started
It's an optical illusion! Ostriches are the largest living birds, but their heads are pretty small. "If you see them picking at the ground from a distance, it may look like their heads are buried in the ground," says Glinda Cunningham of the American Ostrich Association.

Why It's Not True
Ostriches don't bury their heads in the sand - they wouldn't be able to breathe! But they do dig holes in the dirt to use as nests for their eggs. Several times a day, a bird puts her head in the hole and turns the eggs. So it really does look like the birds are burying their heads in the sand!

This is a Blank Page

You May Cut Out Resources On Back

This is a Blank Page

Myth Busters

Author's Point	Author's Reasons and Evidence

This is a Blank Page

You May Cut Out Resources On Back

This is a Blank Page

Two Texts

Directions:
Use the graphic organizers to record important information from two texts on the same topic in order to write or speak about the subject knowledgeably.

Standards: English Language Arts | Informational | RI.4.9

www.CoreCommonStandards.com

This is a Blank Page

You May Cut Out Resources On Back

This is a Blank Page

Two Texts

Important Information from Text #1:
Title: _____

Important Information from Text #2:
Title: _____

This is a Blank Page

You May Cut Out Resources On Back

This is a Blank Page

This is a Blank Page

You May Cut Out Resources On Back

This is a Blank Page

Non-Fiction Fishin'

Directions: Use the graphic organizers to map your thinking as you read non-fiction texts.

The organizers fit texts as follows:
- informational (general)
- history/biography
- social studies (general)
- science (cycle)
- science (general)
- technical

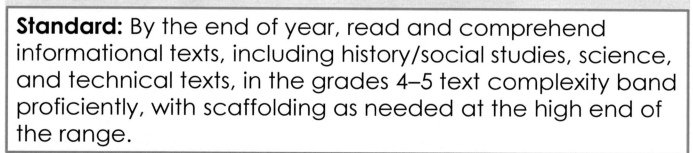

Standard: By the end of year, read and comprehend informational texts, including history/social studies, science, and technical texts, in the grades 4–5 text complexity band proficiently, with scaffolding as needed at the high end of the range.

Standard: English Language Arts | Reading: Informational Text | RI.4.10
Graphics by ScrappinDoodles   www.CoreCommonStandards.com

This is a Blank Page

You May Cut Out Resources On Back

This is a Blank Page

Name_____

Title_____

Author_____

What I **Know**	What I **Want** to Know	What I **Learned**	What I **Still** Want to Learn

Standard: English Language Arts | Reading: Informational Text | RI.4.10

www.CoreCommonStandards.com

This is a Blank Page

You May Cut Out Resources On Back

This is a Blank Page

Name_____

Directions: As you read, summarize four significant events from the text, label the date/year and put them in order on the time line.,

Title_____

Author_____

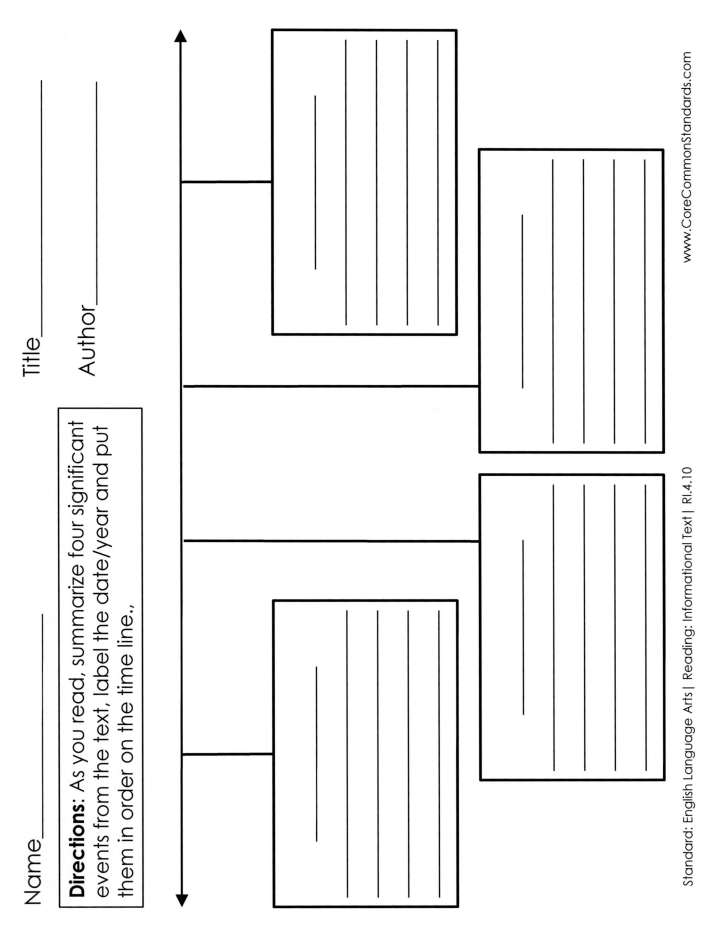

www.CoreCommonStandards.com

Standard: English Language Arts | Reading: Informational Text | RI.4.10

This is a Blank Page

You May Cut Out Resources On Back

This is a Blank Page

Name _____

Title _____

Author _____

Details:

When?

Questions:

Where?

Standard: English Language Arts | Reading: Informational Text | RI.4.10

www.CoreCommonStandards.com

This is a Blank Page

You May Cut Out Resources On Back

This is a Blank Page

Name_____   Title_____

Author_____

Directions: As you read, summarize the parts of a cycle (life cycle, water cycle, etc).

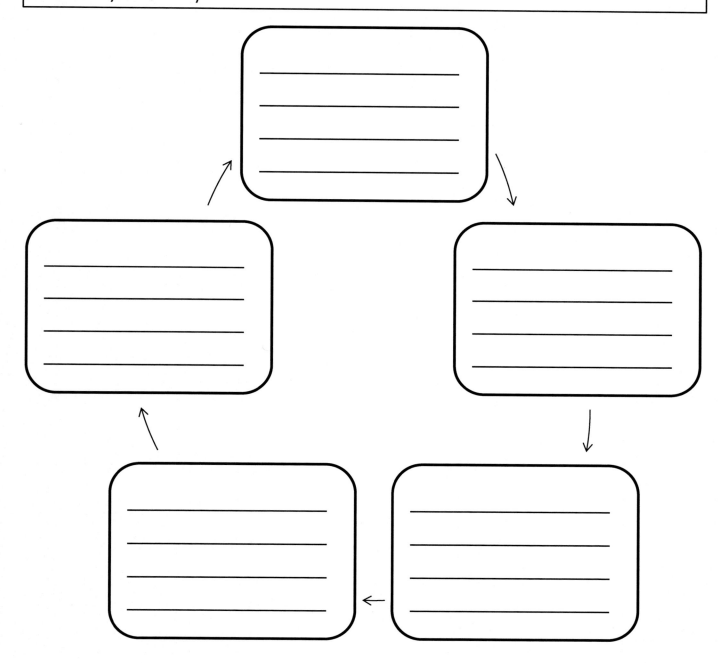

This is a Blank Page

You May Cut Out Resources On Back

This is a Blank Page

Name_____

Title_____

Author_____

Observation	Inference	Why?

Standard: English Language Arts | Reading: Informational Text | RI.4.10

www.CoreCommonStandards.com

This is a Blank Page

You May Cut Out Resources On Back

This is a Blank Page

Name_____   Title_____

Author_____

Directions: As you read, summarize the steps or parts of a technical text (first, next, last).

This is a Blank Page

You May Cut Out Resources On Back

This is a Blank Page

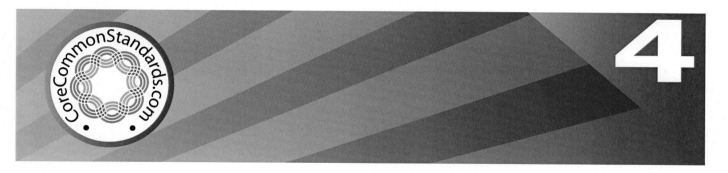

4

Common Core State Standards

Answer Key

Grade 4

•English Standards

Activities that teach every Common Core Standard!

ENGLISH STANDARDS
Pages 5-306

RL.4.1 : Pages 5-20

USE THE TEXT TO MAKE INFERENCES
Use the poster to get hints when making inferences. Read the story and make inferences about characters. A blank page was added to write your own inferences. Answers vary.
Sample answers:
1. Jessie is thrifty. Jessie is not wasteful.
2. Mrs. Johnson is lonely, and Jess wants to be nice to her.
3. Jessie is a good cook. Jessie is good at making pies.
4. Jessie is very busy. Jessie is good at using an opportunity. Jessie is doing good business.
5. Jessie was popular. Jessie was good at what she does.

INFERENCE CHAINS
Use these organizers to make an inference, and then use a direct quote and one more piece of information from the story to support your inference.

RL.4.2 : Pages 21-36

DETERMINING THEME
Read the story. Use the graphic organizer to determine theme. Support with 3 piece of evidence.
Sample Answers...
THEME:
Everyone has their worth, don't judge a book by it's cover, everyone is useful, anyone can be of help...
EVIDENCE:
Eddie usually got picked last.
He wasn't the tallest, biggest, fastest, or slowest kid.
His teammates groaned to see him facing four enemies on his own.
Everyone watched in surprise.
SUMMARY:
Everyone thought Eddie was a bad player. He was picked last, and his teammates expected him to fail. He actually did really well, helped his team out, and won the game!

IDENTIFYING THEMES
Use these cloud card organizers to write about themes. Answers vary according to story chosen.

RL.4.3 : Pages 37-42

WELCOME TO THE NEIGHBORHOOD
Use the graphic organizer to respond to the story. Answers will vary depending on character chosen. This organizer can be reused for any passage or text.

RL.4.4 : Pages 43-80

GREEK MYTHOLOGY
Match the character cards to traits that match them. Practice these skills on the worksheet. Order of the answers in the words and phrases column doesn't matter.

CHARACTER	WORDS & PHRASES	
Hercules	Herculean	Mighty
Achilles	Achilles' Heel	a person's weak spot
Athena	Atheneum	wisdom
King Midas	Midas touch	person who is always lucky
Icarus	wings of wax	don't fly too close to the sun
Medusa	a severely ugly...	turn you to stone...
Orpheus	orphic poems	poet and musician
Odysseus	Odyssey	adventure or journey
Pegasus	winged horse	my Pegasus will not...
Zeus	Mount Olympus	father and ruler...

GREEK MYTHOLOGY
Then write about each character on the character organizer pages. A blank one has also been included for you.

RL.4.5 : Pages 81-116

THREE AMIGOS
Use the original pages as the answer key. Cut out the vocab cards. Sort them into the 3-column chart and copy the words into the venn diagrams, either the 3 circle or 2 circle versions.

IDENTIFYING LITERARY ELEMENTS
Read a story, a poem, and a play. Fill out the literary elements cards. Sort the cards onto the appropriate pile on the sorting page.

RL.4.6 : Pages 117-132

POINT OF VIEW?
Sort the story cards into First and Third points of view. Record your answers on page the worksheet. Correct answers are on the answer key and are repeated here:
FIRST PERSON: B, C, D, G, I , K
THIRD PERSON: A, E, F, H, J, L

RL.4.7 : Pages 133-136

BOOK VS. MOVIE
Compare and contrast a book and a movie on this organizer. Answers vary by topic chosen.

RL.4.9 : Pages 137-144

COMPARE AND CONTRAST ACROSS CULTURES
Compare and contrast the two fables using the Venn Diagram. Answers Vary.

RL.4.10 : Pages 145-158

THINKING MAPS FOR READING JOURNEYS
Use these different graphic organizers to respond to text.

RI.4.1 : Pages 159-168

HURRICANES
Use the hint cards while reading the story. Then answer the questions.
1. A
2. B
3. D
4. B
5. D
6. B
7. C
8. A

RI.4.2 : Pages 169-174

WHAT'S THE MAIN IDEA?
Read the story about poison dart frogs. Use the organizer to write down the main idea, supporting details, and a summary. There is a second version of the story with a new graphic organizer and a longer summary paper, as well.
Sample answers...
MAIN IDEA: Poison Dart frogs are very interesting. Poison Dart Frogs are very different from regular frogs we know.
SUPPORTING DETAILS: They have enough poison to kill 10 men. They are very colorful. They carry children on their back like monkeys. Scientists don't know why they are so poisonous. Scientists are trying to make medicine from their poisons.
SUMMARY: *answers vary*

RI.4.3 : Pages 175-180

WHY, OH WHY?
Read the story. Use the graphic organizer to show cause and effect events from the story. This organizer can be reused with other texts, too.

RI.4.4 : Pages 181-250

JEOPARDY
Play the Jeopardy game. Match the answers to the questions in the different categories. Copy answers for at least 5 questions on the worksheet. Answers are included.

RI.4.5 : Pages 251-264

DIGGING FOR INFORMATION
Use this variety of graphic organizers to organize information found in text.

RI.4.6 : Pages 265-272

FIRSTHAND AND SECONDHAND ACCOUNTS
Read these or two other passages and use the graphic organizers to compare and contrast firsthand and secondhand accounts of the same events.

RI.4.7 : Pages 273-278

CONTRIBUTIONS TO THE TEXT
Use the graphic organizers provided to describe how pictures, motion, speech, or other audio/visual elements add to the presentation. The suggested material is Roosevelt's Address after Pearl Harbor.

RI.4.8 : Pages 279-286

ANIMAL MYTH BUSTERS
Read the stories and write some main points with evidence on the organizer.
Sample answers...
Toads don't give you warts - they come from a virus. They do have some poisons though.
Ostriches don't put their heads in the sand - they do turn eggs, and they do dig in the ground though.

RI.4.9 : Pages 287-292

TWO TEXTS
Compare two texts with these graphic organizers.

RI.4.10 : Pages 293-306

NON-FICTION FISHIN'
Use this variety of graphic organizers to summarize what you have read.

Common Core State Standards
Educating classrooms one standard at a time.

Made in the USA
Middletown, DE
02 June 2015